Language in America

John Tinkler

Language in America

Edited by
Neil Postman, Charles Weingartner, and
Terence P. Moran

PEGASUS   NEW YORK

Acknowledgments

The editors of this volume are grateful to the Coordinating Council of Literary Magazines whose grant to *Monocle* helped make this book possible. And they are also grateful to *Monocle Magazine,* an occasional journal of political irreverence, for suggesting this inquiry into language in America and giving us the freedom to follow our own inclinations, reverent or otherwise. "The Language of Bureaucracy" by Henry A. Barnes used with permission from Mrs. Henry A. Barnes.

Introduction

> ... Words are indispensable but also can be fatal—the only
> begetters of all civilization, all science, all consistency of
> high purpose, all angelic goodness, and the only begetters
> at the same time of all superstition, all collective madness
> and stupidity, all worse-than-bestial diabolism, all the
> dismal historical succession of crimes in the name of God,
> King, Nation, Party, Dogma. Never before, thanks to the
> techniques of mass communication, have so many listeners
> been so completely at the mercy of so few speakers. Never
> have misused words—those hideously efficient tools of all
> the tyrants, warmongers, persecutors, and heresy-hunters—
> been so widely and disastrously influential as they are
> today. Generals, clergymen, advertisers, and the rulers of
> totalitarian states—all have good reasons for disliking the
> idea of universal education in the rational use of language.
> To the military, clerical, propagandist, and authoritarian
> mind such training seems (and rightly seems) profoundly
> subversive.
>
> Aldous Huxley
> "Education on the Nonverbal Level"
> *Daedalus,* Spring 1962

Language is commonly referred to as man's most distinctive
achievement. But as Huxley's quote suggests, language is not
exactly an unmixed blessing. It is, in fact, something of a
Faustian bargain, giving and taking away at the same time.
When language takes away more than it gives, books like the
one before you become necessary.

As presumptuous as it may sound, this book is about human
survival. Man, along with all other forms of life, is committed
to surviving. The first level of survival—physical—occupies
virtually all of the time and much of the effort of *all* forms
of life. Many forms of life can "think," but only man, through
symbols, can think about thinking. Or, to put it another way,
man is the only form of life with the potential for *abstracting,*
for using symbols to stand for aspects of the existential environment in which he tries to survive. This permits him to
transcend space-time. He is free to move, symbolically, back-

ward or forward in time. The ability to code and store knowledge in verbal symbols permits man to "know" more than is coded in his DNA chain. But what he can get to "know" can be more a threat to his survival than a means of ensuring it. For example, it sometimes happens that what men know through their verbal symbols is at such great variance with their subverbal, genetic knowledge that they get sick and even die. Consider, for instance, what we commonly call fear. All forms of animal life have coded in the genes subverbal knowledge which can be called survival strategies. Fear is one such strategy. In the face of a threat to its survival, a living organism attains instant readiness by an incredibly complex series of reactions. On the nonverbal level (through what we call the autonomic nervous system), a variety of processes occurs—in humans as in other animal life. These processes can be described only in the most simple-minded ways since our language cannot begin to code the complexity and speed of the processes. The way we say it goes something like this: The "old brain" (preverbal) is "coded" (genetically) to set off a series of systems inside the animal. Chemicals, such as adrenalin, are pumped from the endocrine system into the bloodstream, which (1) accelerates the rate of circulation of the blood by speeding up heart action, (2) simultaneously primes the blood to coagulate more quickly than normal, (3) speeds up the movement of the diaphragm to accelerate breathing, (4) causes perspiration to enable the cooling to normal limits of the organism operating at high speed, etc.

This happens in *all* animals when "fear" is induced. The preverbal purpose of all of this activity is to ready the animal to survive through one of the "classic" forms of survival activity: (1) to fight the threat to survival, or (2) to flee from it. The organism can persist in this "state of emergency" for only brief periods. A prolonged state of fear can be maintained only at great physical cost. Most animals—other than man—need to resort to survival activity on this level only episodically, and even then for only brief periods, until the threat is defeated or "deleted" (by fleeing from it). Man, of course, can use language to aid him in perceiving threats that his preverbal systems could not apprehend. But man is also capable of using language to invent threats and to keep himself in a chronic state of fear. When he does, he suffers all of the consequences of this most unnatural state. In other words, part of the price that man pays for his language-using ability is that he responds to threats that exist *only because* he can verbally transcend a given point in space-time, and symbolically construct and sustain threats to himself. It is equally true that through language man is able to persuade himself that he is in no great danger when, in fact, he is on the brink of annihilation.

Language, then, is the key to human survival. It is, as Korzybski said, our map for charting what is happening both inside and outside of our skins. When the map is inaccurate or inappropriate, our chances of survival are decreased. And not only at the physical level. We can talk ourselves into emotional death, or moral insensibility. We can even impose on language the Sisyphean task of exorcising the demon of uncertainty. Indeed, it may be that this is the primary and most dangerous function of all human symbols—to create the illusion of security in an environment of unremitting change.

In any case, it is clear that with and through language man codes the realities in which he must survive. It is equally clear that language is man's unique instrument for survival—at any level—if he knows that it is and if he constantly checks the results it produces.

This book is intended to serve as a check on some of the many "languages" currently being used in America to codify reality. Each of the contributors was asked to address himself to the general question, To what extent is the language of (politics / advertising / psychotherapy / education / bureaucracy / etc.) facilitating or impeding our chances of survival? Each has answered in his own way, with varying degrees of optimism/pessimism. Without exception, there is deep concern in each of these "status reports" that a mode of discourse has somehow got out of control, that it is not doing for us what it is intended to do, and that our mutual survival strategies are therefore losing some of their potency. But there is also a feeling that, as Huxley expressed it, through a universal education in the rational use of language there is hope that we may restore some balance to our Faustian bargain. The schools do not seem interested in such an effort (too subversive, perhaps). And so we have tried in this volume to make a beginning toward monitoring the language environment. We do not claim that we have been exhaustive. Nor do we claim that our judgments or those of our contributors are necessarily the best "reading" of the "languages" we have dealt with. We do claim that what we have put together is *necessary,* and is in fact, a kind of survival strategy in itself.

Contents

Demeaning of Meaning
Or, What's the Language-Pollution Index Today?

Neil Postman

Shortly after Martin Luther King was assassinated (or was it Bobby Kennedy?), Lyndon Johnson told the nation that he didn't believe in violence. Eric Sevareid said the same thing. So did Hubert Humphrey, Walter Cronkite, Harry Reasoner, and just about every other person who had access to the public ear and eye. Stokely Carmichael was an exception. He made it clear that he *does* believe in violence. *The New York Times* led one to believe he is crazy.

Of course, Lyndon Johnson did not exactly *mean* that he doesn't believe in violence. Neither did the others. What they meant to say was that they don't believe in violence when it is directed at them. When violence is directed at people they don't like, its commission is regarded as a matter of national honor. Check with Captain Levy.

Now, we are dealing here with a very serious problem, although not quite the problem you might suppose. There is nothing unusual about an American president opting for violence. Heads of state rarely consider viable any other method of resolving what they construe to be their troubles. No one but a dizzy romantic expects this to change in the near future. But if it is ever to change, or, more realistically, if we are to resolve some of our more reachable moral, social, and political problems, we will require, as a precondition, a relatively clean semantic environment. Thus, the most immediate danger to our survival is not that Lyndon Johnson, or *The New York Times,* or Walter Cronkite believes in the virtue of well-directed, effective violence, but that they *say* they do not. The effect of many people saying what in fact they do not believe is that the semantic environment becomes polluted. And a badly polluted semantic environment means that language is an unreliable instrument for human com-

13

munication, and therefore not reliable for the resolution of human problems.

As in the case of air and water pollution, the menace of language pollution increases in direct proportion to the increase in the volume of garbage. There have always been men who have used language as a means of concealing, deceiving, and expressing their ignorance, just as men have always urinated in fresh streams. A stream can tolerate, absorb, even convert to good uses a certain amount of waste. So can the semantic environment. But beyond a given bulk, garbage creates an ecological imbalance. The built-in survival strategies of the environment are overcome. It sickens and becomes useless.

In considering the ecology of the semantic environment, we must take into account what is called the communications revolution. The invention of new and various media of communication has given a voice and an audience to many people whose opinions would otherwise not be solicited, and who, in fact, have little if anything to contribute to public issues. Many of these people are entertainers, such as Johnny Carson, Hugh Downs, Joey Bishop, David Susskind, Ronald Reagan, Barbara Walters, and Joe Garagiola. Before the communications revolution, their public utterances would have been limited almost exclusively to sentences composed by more knowledgeable people, or they would have had no opportunity to make public utterances at all. Things being what they are, the press and air waves are filled with the featured and prime-time sentences of people who are in no position to render informed judgments on what they are talking about: like Joey Bishop on the sociological implications of drugs, Johnny Carson on educational innovation, Ronald Reagan on the *Pueblo* incident, David Susskind on anything, and Hugh Downs on menopause. ("It is," he says, "a controversial subject.").

Another problem created by the communications revolution is generated by the sheer bulk of the media. Even if the press, radio, and TV were largely devoted to the dissemination of opinions of our most well-informed citizens, a substantial amount of garbage would still be present. Even smart people run out of smart things to say—in fact, usually sooner than they anticipate. But if one must write a column every day, or an article every week, or answer complicated questions in thirty seconds, one is soon responsible for more nonsense than can be retracted in a lifetime. In other words, big media demand lots of stuff, fast, and they don't especially discriminate among the kinds of stuff.

A third problem of the media is produced by their collective intensity. A single medium, no matter how filled with waste, will not usually contaminate the semantic environment. But when there is a saturation of nonsense from many media at the same time, the effect is toxic.

It is important to say that the big media are not the only source of semantic contamination, and even if they were, it would be irrelevant to declare oneself "against" the communications revolution. That would be the equivalent of declaring oneself against the roads and highways that make it possible for many people to spend time in the country, where they will leave behind a trail of beer cans. The roads are here to stay. So are the media. What this means is that we must learn how to protect our precious environments.

Consider what follows, then, an attempt to describe the characteristics of a reasonably healthy semantic environment. My remarks are addressed to those whose lives are touched by the problem.

Let us define a semantic environment as any human situation in which language plays a critical role. This means that the constituents of the environment are (1) people, (2) their purposes, and (3) the language they use to help them achieve their purposes. Because there are so many different human purposes, there are, of course, many different kinds of semantic environments. Science is a semantic environment. So is politics; commerce; war; love-making; praying; reporting; law-making; etc. Each of these situations is a context in which people want to do something to, for, with, or against other people, and in which the communication of meaning (language) plays a decisive role. *A healthy semantic environment is one in which language effectively serves the purposes of the particular context in which it is used.* "Effectively" means here that language is useful in helping people understand what their purposes are, what functions their activity serves, and what needs they are trying to satisfy. The semantic environment is polluted when people do not trust and cannot use the "language" of a particular human context. The semantic environment is polluted when language obscures from people what they are doing and why they are doing it.

The following illustrations are intended to give a clearer understanding of how semantic pollution works:

(1) The language of science, like other "languages," has several functions, but none more important than the communication of statements about the world from an "objective," detached, and verifiable point of view. At its purest, the language of science is public information. It is tentative (never to be accepted as gospel), and it is relatively free of ambiguity. The language of science begins to become polluted when it is used to communicate subjective, self-serving, ambiguous, or private meanings. For example, pollution occurs when the language of science (a) is used to perpetuate a particular social doctrine (as by Stalin); (b) becomes "classified" and, therefore, private (as by the Pentagon and American universities); (c) is used to further someone's economic interests (as by the tobacco industry); (d) is used by people who do not understand its referents or its methods of validation (as by television entertainers who say, "Science has proven beyond a doubt . . ."); (e) is used for purposes it is not intended to serve ("Did you see that gorgeous sunset last evening?" "The sun did not, strictly speaking, *set* last evening or any other evening. If anything, one ought to say that the earth rose. In any case, the sun is in a relatively fixed position in relation to the earth.")

I do not wish to imply that objective, detached, unambiguous, public, and tentative language is good *in itself* (as the saying goes). It is "good" in the context of the human activity called science. "Good" means it does what it is supposed to do in that context. The language of science is "bad" in a number of other human contexts, most assuredly in the process of love-making, where language in order to be good (do what it's supposed to) must be personal, emotional, private, and categorical.

(2) The language of religion has (and has had) many different purposes. For most of man's history, the language of religion was used in much the same way as we presently use the language of science. For precisely that reason most of humanity was unable to find out very much about the world and, as a consequence, was retarded in developing, among other things, its technology. One of man's greatest discoveries was that the language of religion is an inappropriate medium for the rigorous exploration of the natural environment. Once that discovery was made, it was inevitable we would land safely on the moon. One might say that the language of religion became polluted at exactly that point in antiquity when men used it to provide literal explanations of the world rather than as metaphors for their most deeply rooted feelings of loneliness. The pollution worsened when men contrived to use the language of religion as a vehicle of political coercion. When myths become dogma the result is a totalitarian politics, from which humanity has been struggling for centuries to free itself. What I am assuming is this: At its purest, the language of religion has as its main purpose the construction of metaphors which give concrete form to humanity's most profound fears and exaltations. It serves to minimize fear, to increase freedom, and to provide a sense of continuity and oneness. Thus, when the language of religion is sectarian, coercive, and literal, it is polluted. Examples of recent filtering processes are: (a) the Catholic Church's recent efforts to de-mythologize itself (that is, exorcise literalism); (b) the Church's effort to make its constituents "forget" the traditional, liturgical condemnation of the Jews (that is, minimize sectarianism); (c) the Supreme Court's ruling against the enforced recitation of prayers in the public schools (that is, reduce coercion).

(3) In a democratic society, the language of politics has as one of its main purposes the clear statement of practical, alternative ways of living. In a healthy semantic environment,

citizens understand what these alternatives are. They understand them because their representatives have stated them
with as little ambiguity as possible. In a healthy environment,
citizens also believe that the alternative articulated by a
political leader is, in fact, the alternative he believes in. For
example, if a man says he is in favor of an open-housing law
and that he wants his constituents to consider carefully his
reasons, it must be taken for granted that he, at least, believes
in the wisdom of such a law. If citizens do not believe what
their political leaders say, the language of politics is polluted
(not doing what it's supposed to). Moreover, since a major
function of political language is to express *practical* ways of
living, it is essential that political language be fairly accurate
in its representation of "reality." There is no greater threat
to the ecological balance of the political-semantic environment
than language that is unrelated to external realities. In our
own country, examples of this are abundant: (a) categorizing
the world into two groups: "free and enslaved," "open and
closed," "Communist and non-Communist," etc.; (b) using
euphemisms to obscure the nature of political or military
activity: "Operation Sunshine" (for hydrogen-bomb tests),
"liberating" villages (for killing their inhabitants), "military
advisers" (for soldiers), "saving" towns (for destroying them);
(c) using and fixating on inappropriate metaphors: the Communist Conspiracy, the Domino Theory, the Monroe Doctrine,
"winning" the war, etc.; (d) lying: the Gulf of Tonkin affair,
The *Pueblo* incident, etc.

I trust it is clear that I am not attempting to state all the
conditions in which these "languages" are demeaned. In order
to do that, one would have to provide a full description of
the manifold purposes of each "language" and then note all
those instances in which these purposes are trespassed on,
undermined, even obliterated by one semantic device or another. But such a thorough analysis is not required to recognize that the semantic-pollution index is rising. For example,
one does not need to be an expert on the language of the law
to understand that it differs strikingly from the language of
literary criticism. What, then, shall we make of the fact that

the severity of the sentence given LeRoi Jones seemed to be related to the presiding judge's low opinion of Jones's poetry? A thorough analysis of the language of advertising is not needed to acknowledge that no legitimate human purposes are served by language intended to persuade people that cigarette smoking is a *healthful* practice. ("You can take Salem out of the country, but you can't take the country out of Salem.") No expert on the language of news reporting is needed to understand that there are creeping racist overtones in the statement, "Cassius Clay, who prefers to be known as Muhammad Ali. . . ." Have you ever heard a reporter say, "Bernard Schwartz, who prefers to be known as Tony Curtis . . ."?

Of course, the protection of our semantic environments does require expertise. But even more, it requires concern. The essays in this book are intended to express and arouse concern about the quality of our semantic environment. Perhaps they may even stimulate action. Toward that end, here are some suggestions, both practical and bizarre, for those concerned with our semantic environment to reflect upon:

(1) The most bizarre possibility of all is that our schools will take seriously such an idea as expressed in Huxley's quote at the beginning of the Introduction to this book, and provide an education in the rational use of language. Such an effort would require teachers to take a serious interest in reality. That requirement, all by itself, bars any hope that our schools can become an important ally in the task of filtering our semantic environment. Nonetheless, interested readers might wish to write to school administrators, visit classes, examine textbooks, and otherwise embarrass educators into acknowledging the role of language in human affairs.

(2) Interested readers might wish to urge their representatives to consider the establishment of a Cabinet post concerned with preserving and enriching our semantic environment. Naturally, I do *not* have in mind anything remotely resembling the Academy in France. As the line goes, "The French don't care what they say, actually, as long as it's pronounced correctly." I am talking about an institution that

would be concerned exclusively with what people are *saying*, not with their pronunciations and grammatical constructions. Perhaps S. I. Hayakawa could be appointed our first Secretary of the Language Environment. His office might produce a weekly publication, something similar to Consumer Reports, that would provide the most current examples of semantic pollution, including his own.

(3) We might work to establish a National Language-Pollution Filtering Week. During that week, everyone would be urged to confine his remarks to matters that concern only the barest necessities of living. The rest would be silence. Perhaps in this way we could help ourselves to achieve a healthier perspective on what language is for and how precious its sensible uses are.

(4) There is a requirement that, I believe, goes something like this: When an actor is portraying a physician on, say, a television commercial, some indication of this fact must be given to the audience. The usual form is to flash on the screen the words THIS IS A DRAMATIZATION. Similarly, the FCC might require that whenever someone totally unqualified to speak on a subject does so, with impunity (that is, without acknowledging his lack of expertise), there must be flashed on the screen the words THIS PERSON DOES NOT KNOW WHAT HE IS TALKING ABOUT.

(5) Perhaps magazines and newspapers can be encouraged to feature regular analyses of the semantic environment. A sort of expanded version of the *Times's* Quotation of the Day. These might be called "Dumb Statements of the Day." Two- or three-paragraph commentaries on these statements might be sufficient to help reduce their number.

(6) Finally, can you imagine TV newscasts ending each night with an estimate of the language-pollution index? Right after the weather man would come the language man. "Thank you, Tom. Today the language-pollution index rose to the danger point and the Governor had to request that a period of silence be imposed starting at 6 P.M. this evening. He lifted the ban at 10 this evening, and tomorrow's prospects for a healthier day seem quite good."

Telling It Like It Is

From the Associated Press:

"WASHINGTON, March 16, 1968—President Johnson told a news conference last week that there was 'no truth' to reports that he was looking for a successor to Henry Cabot Lodge as ambassador to South Vietnam. White House Press Secretary George Christian was asked about this today. He said Johnson's statement of March 9 was absolutely accurate—that the President had already picked Ambassador-at-Large Ellsworth Bunker to succeed Lodge."

General Lewis Hershey before a House committee in June 1966:

"I do not want to go along on a volunteer basis. I think a fellow should be compelled to become better and not use his discretion whether he wants to get smarter, more healthy, or more honest."

From U. S. Marine Corps Platoon Book:

"The cold skill of effectively wielded bayonet-tipped rifles in hand-to-hand combat produces a vastly demoralizing psychological effect on enemy troops."

From a Hilton ad in *Life:*

"Now the whole country is open for exploration. From star-watching in Hollywood to show-stopping in New York City. From Dixieland jazz in New Orleans to a symphony in Boston. Just stay with Hilton. And the country is yours in one attractive, bargain-priced package."

The Language of Politics

Geoffrey Wagner

> When the general atmosphere is bad, language must suffer.
>
> George Orwell, *Politics and the English Language*

Nightmare is compounded of the failure of assumption. A floor fails to support the walker, clothing comes alive, stones liquefy, the tongue turns into a centipede writhing inside the mouth, a whole city starts throbbing—all elements in the "panic" vision of Antoine Roquentin in Sartre's *La Nausée,* which, though published as fiction in 1938, well described actual conditions in bombed Hiroshima later.

The crisis of political discourse in American life, indeed in Western life, pertains to nightmare since it involves a threat, as it were behind our backs, to habits of spatial and social thinking. So complex in appearance that every refuge seems vain, and threatening all stability of existence in that it menaces the very duty of language itself to keep us human, this dilemma may yet be simply stated: political language both asks to be translated and yet, by its nature, cannot be. It is not sign language, it never says what it means; George Orwell remarked, "In the case of a word like *democracy,* not only is there no agreed definition, but the attempt to make one is resisted from all sides."

In this we see, first and foremost, the potential dishonesty of a language system. Or rather, of the perversion of a language system. Speaking at the June 1964 P.E.N. Congress in Oslo, R. F. Thanh Lang of Vietnam described the rape of language by politics as a principally Occidental phenomenon:

> In Vietnam, for instance, those beautiful terms—peace, liberty, democracy, equality—were imported into our country by Westerners at the end of the nineteenth century ... in fact, we were much freer, and more democratic, before we had the good fortune to be able to pronounce these

words with our mouths; and today if you utter such words
in front of any Vietnamese, he will simply give you a
good-natured smile. For a Vietnamese liberty means: Liberty to go to prison. . . .[1]

To say that this development endangers our survival is the
understatement of the atomic era, and our task must be
resolutely to identify the anti-human symptoms which are
steering our language off course. For meaning is dependent
on an organization of various elements, including what is *not*
said. The meaning of a word, in I. A. Richards' well-known
formulation, is the missing part of its context. "When you
think of a concrete object," Orwell wrote in 1946, "you think
wordlessly."

In a society without true liberty, man submits to this
situation rather in the manner of a neurotic whose neurosis
is its own symptoms. He learns to "live with himself." It is
because political utterances about democracy and so forth
demand to be translated that politicians choose woolly language, on a high level of abstraction, behind which they may
maneuver. The American Constitution happens to be a
masterpiece of applicable abstraction, full of active verbs and
created out of direct visual images. Clear thinking demands
mental images. It is far easier to obfuscate meaning and to
use *democracy* as a vague term of approval rather than a
specific way of acting.

I well remember sitting listening to the famous Eisen-
hower-Macmillan "debate" of the mid-fifties. After about a
quarter of an hour my wife remarked with a frown, "They
must say something soon." But they didn't. And a subsequent
inspection of the transcript revealed that no real context *could*
define the verbal situations created. (I have had the same
sensation listening to the rhetoric of Ayn Rand.) To set words
in a unitary mold at odds with the parts of speech of which

---

[1] R. F. Thanh Lang, Session Four, reprinted in *Arena,* No. 24, October
1965, pp. 58–59. (My trans.) With the last comment, compare Orwell's Newspeak Appendix to *1984:* "The word *free* still existed in Newspeak, but it could
only be used in such statements as 'This dog is free from lice' or 'This field
is free from weeds.'"

it is composed is the characteristic afflatus of technological office today. By its construction alone it cannot convey meaning, let alone truth. This is what caused Orwell to comment that in most political discourse today "one is not watching a live human being but some kind of dummy."

Written at the end of the last war, Orwell's essay "Politics and the English Language" states his recognition of the danger of dissociated personality and reduced consciousness implicit in modern political utterance. He suggested what Thanh Lang stated some twenty years later, that Western political utterance is *per se* a rupture of the symbiotic bond, in which (to paraphrase Thanh Lang) the sign and the thing signified betray each other; what demands to be translated cannot be translated and language poisons itself with its own vomit.

Orwell condensed this well: "In our time, political speech and writing are largely the defense of the indefensible." He cited British rule in India, the Russian purges, and the atom bomb. In short, you cannot tell your constituency or district that you are dropping burning petroleum jelly on a group of Asiatics beside whose flag you were raising your own a few years back. You simply cannot say aloud, in public, that you are deporting Asiatic peasantry en masse and at gunpoint, burning their houses and crops, and herding them into insanitary concentration camps. Instead, you say that you are resettling a number of *refugees*. When I heard General Westmoreland's address to Congress in 1967, I realized the force of Orwell's point. Indeed, a good exercise in verbal sincerity is to give a group of students the task of writing one of the speeches of the President, on a given subject, before he delivers it. The language will be bound to be question-begging and soporifically vague, so that an intelligent student can sometimes provide whole paragraphs in advance. The humor of Twain's story "Buck Fanshaw's Funeral" is based on this problem of lexical translation of jargon and pleonasm.

It is perhaps the case that English is particularly susceptible to political jargon. Both Orwell and "Q" (Sir Arthur Quiller-Couch) independently thought so. It is generally composed of roundabout or inflated phraseology, of a plethora of suffixes, the overuse of copulative verbs, and the tell-tale substitution of the passive for the active. In the active and transitive verb forms you are responsible, not somebody else: the Gettysburg Address is almost wholly active.

Such jargon flourishes when the behavior of society is of the same order of motive as that which generates a divorce from reality. Roosevelt was apparently forever unscrambling governmental newspeak. A Public Administration blackout order of 1942 ran:

> Such preparations shall be made as will completely obscure all Federal buildings and non-federal buildings occupied by the Federal Government during an air-raid for any period of time from visibility by reason of internal or external illumination.

Roosevelt derobotized this to: "Tell them that in buildings where they have to keep the work going, to put something across the windows," a particularly heartening revision of official gobbledegook since it is nongrammatical, containing an "open" noun clause of the kind a freshman English instructor sees it his mission to massacre. Despite eccentric syntax the meaning still comes briskly across. Orwell did the reverse with Ecclesiastes' "I returned and saw under the sun . . ." ("Objective consideration of contemporary phenomena compels the conclusion . . .").[2]

Western political jargon remains a pure perversion of language in that it is a linguistically fictitious entity proper to robots rather than men. In suggesting that English accommodates this kind of jargon with greater facility than most

[2] Another transliteration of the sort involved an immigrant plumber who wrote to the Federal Bureau of Standards about the excellence of hydrochloric acid in clearing drains. The Bureau's reply, "The efficacy of hydrochloric acid is indisputable, but the corrosive residue is incompatible with metallic permanence," had eventually to be modified to, "DON'T USE HYDROCHLORIC ACID. IT EATS HELL OUT OF THE PIPES." Richard Altick attributes this anecdote to the Dean of M.I.T. (*Preface to Critical Reading,* New York: Henry Holt, 1951, p. 87), but I must say I heard it years before when working as press officer for Imperial Chemical Industries.

Official obfuscation by acronym is another prevalent form of nontalk and deserves an article to itself.

other languages (except perhaps German),[3] I had in mind the persuasive theory, first expounded by Dolf Sternberger in his *Aus dem Wörterbuch des Unmenschen* (1945), and developed in Cornelia Berning's 1965 *Vom "Abstammungsnachweis" zum "Zuchtwart,"* that German grammar was such at the time that Nazi politics lodged easily within the language itself. It is almost certain that a given language transmits some thoughts more easily than others, and one linguist, Bernard Karlgren, believes that when the Chinese abandon their script, with its depth relation to knowledge, they will in effect abandon their culture. Today, as they say, optimists learn Russian, pessimists Chinese.

In any event it is curiously the case that the rupture in the symbolic process involved in our current political discourse is proceeding as a policy in many American classrooms. A recent national Commission of English, established by the College Entrance Board, reported, "*Macbeth* vies with the writing of thank-you notes for time in the curriculum." And why not? To turn Hamlet's famous summation of the supernatural into "The universe, Horatio, contains many wonders that the science you are addicted to has never even imagined as yet" is to introduce the student most usefully to contemporary jargon. He will be able to behave well in a bank. How recognizable today is the celebrated reflection on suicide— "Shall I continue to live or not? This is the momentous question I am called upon to make." Here the tedious original has everywhere been conflated into contemporary Eisenhowerese.[4]

---

[3] A recent study of problems of translation suggests that such is indeed the case: Fritz Güttinger, *Zielsprache: Theorie und Technik des Übersetzens,* Zürich, Manesse Verlag, 1963.

[4] The Ghost's speech in I, v, is Eisenhowered by the Coles' Everyday English series to the following: "Were it not that I am compelled to remain silent concerning the nature of my place of correction, I could give an account, the most trifling detail of which would acutely distress your mind, congeal your youthful blood, cause your organs of vision to shoot wildly from their orbits, and each individual hair of your matted and tangled ringlets to spring up and remain erect, as the spikes of the porcupine do when that animal is irritated."

It is this assault on the nature of language itself which has lately initiated a cynicism toward verbal communication as a whole in our young. "To say a word 'means' something," writes the British legal semanticist Arthur Owen Barfield, "implies that it means that same something more than once." If government spokesmen use a word to symbolize X one day ("advisers . . . technicians") and Y the next (Thunderchief bombers), they are playing Russian roulette with the human race. Language gets viewed as an irritating ancillary on the road to dominance. This defiling of words is a human treason, and benumbs our sensibilities until we can coin terms like *overkill* and *peace offensive.*

The speech figure represented by such terms is an oxymoron, combining contradictory referents, e.g., *darkness visible* (Milton), *noiseless noise* (Keats). So we have had the *clean bomb,* and *safe accidents* (in an investigation into auto safety). But a hyperbole like *overkill* was employed by Shakespeare only for characters who were, if not actually insane, at least pushed close to neurotic by emotional situations: Othello asked to have Cassio "nine years a-killing" (*overkill*). In a 1966 ballot *yes* was deformed to mean *no* when New York City voters had to vote *yes* if they were against civilian review boards for the police, and *no* if they wanted to express, Yes, we'd like them.

If the student generation is today the new power elite (*pace* Paul Goodman), the superiority lies in their resistance to the word-world of their elders, or what is called the Incredibility Crap. However shaky, Margaret Schlauch's theory of the growth of language paralleling the psychic development of the individual suggests that the postadolescent is particularly able to identify the residue of the irrational in speech habits. The average age of an American as I write is twenty-six, and growing younger; it is said that half of all speakers of American English are now adolescents.

This average student was born during the Korean "police action" (the term was Harry Truman's), in which there were 33,629 American battle deaths and 157,530 (*light?*) casualties, and which was subsequently redefined as a *war* by an Appellate Court, to the undiluted joy of insurance companies, who exclude from their policies losses resulting from war or insurrection.

Our average student has thus known *cold war* all his life, and a draft, politely euphemized as *selective service* (a "selection" he declines at his peril). Unlike most Europeans of his age he has heard air-raid sirens tested all his life, banshee wailings that misalert biochemical body timings, he has seen complacent ads for bomb-shelter comforts in his glossy magazines,[5] and has been told on the side that an illegal war is a patriotic duty; he has bent his head to his President's saying, "Our purpose is not war but peace,"[6] made while bombers were raiding Haiphong and Hanoi. Perhaps he remembers his Shakespeare:

> Then let us say you are sad,
> Because you are not merry; and twere as easy
> For you to laugh, and leap, and say you are merry,
> Because you are not sad.[7]

The word *peace* is totally fractured when it is forced to contain within itself children and old people horribly burned and maimed. We bomb the Vietcong because "Our honor is at stake." This kind of semantic inversion, then, is reminiscent of the preacher at the drive-in church who is said to have said, "Your prayers are answered. Because whatever happens, that's the answer." Today's student remains undeceived. He has noted a respected university historian and ex-presidential adviser declaring to a reporter who confronted him with an objective lie (concerning the Bay of Pigs invasion), "Did I say that? Oh, that was the cover story." In May 1965 the same

---

[5] "BOMB SHELTER CANDLE—Burns 4 Days—Contains Air Freshener—Deodorant—$2.50 each, 2 for $4.90 ppd. SHELTER SPECIFICATIONS REQUIRE CANDLES—satisfaction guaranteed." (Advertisement from Jack and Jane Hicks, Southern Pines, North Carolina) One wonders who will make good the guarantee should Jack 'n' Jane not be around when the deodorant fails.

[6] Des Moines, Iowa, July 1, 1966.

[7] *The Merchant of Venice,* I, sc. i, ll. 47-50.

student observed the New York State Assembly triumphantly defeating *ethics legislation* and was no doubt reminded, during this same month, that he must not cheat on examinations.

Thanh Lang tells us that the Vietnamese word for propaganda, *puin jen,* is interchangeable with the word for a *lie.* Of course, the word *propaganda* is almost equally poisoned in our own tongue, but it is Thanh Lang's contention that literary symbolism (*"On dit une chose et fait penser à une autre chose"*) is destroyed when used to deceive, as our advertising deliberately deceives, rather than to aid and assist man to survive.

Sartre, too, knew how the true magic of words (such as night, light, water) could be corrupted by the inverted symbol relationships of modern urban man—"All they have ever seen is trained water running from taps, light which fills bulbs when you turn on the switch. . . ." The Janus effect is suggested by Hollywood at night: along the segment of Sunset Boulevard known as Sunset Strip there is so much light at night, from floodlit facades and driveways, not to mention swimming pools and patios and serial-flashing rear lights and trucks lit up as if for some inexistent Christmas on the freeways, that it is night itself which seems artificial. The recoil mechanism of language has gone into effect. At the last New York World's Fair there was a frontage that lit up, patriotically enough, every time an American was born (Equitable Life Assurance). The whole affair seemed pure self-parody, or so much Terry Southern satire: one envisaged the bulb lit and the American born thereafter. The cult of Bob Dylan no longer seems in the slightest eccentric. Apart from turning his back on the betrayals of ritual communication of the political nature, Dylan sang us a gravelly ballad, *On the Eve of Destruction,* in which we were enjoined to "think of all the hate in Red China" and to consider that "human respect is disintegrating"; it reads today like a fairly literal description of our condition—as the targets for escalation run out in Vietnam.

Yet this is not the worst. The way in which we allow ourselves to use this terminology of inexistence is possibly the most telling temperature chart of our time. Verbal disguise, or euphemism, is semantically self-protective. Unpleasant realities are mercifully beclouded—a *tumor* is more bearable than *cancer.* To tell someone he is *crippled,* or *deformed,* is clearly more brutal than to suggest he is *handicapped;* after all, a sports player in the best of health is sometimes *handicapped,* thus to be blind is simply to be *visually handicapped.*

In this spirit, Nebraska's Hospital for the Crippled and Deformed is now the Nebraska Orthopedic Hospital, while the old New York Hospital for the Society for the Relief of the Ruptured and Crippled was retitled—mercifully in all senses— the Hospital for Special Surgery. Mencken once investigated or, rather, listed this sort of thing, and I have myself adduced to the same point the new rhetoric of prosthodontics (largely speaking, the amelioration of supposedly repulsive dental references).[8] You could not, it seemed to me, buttonhole an honest-to-God prosthodontist and say, "Care for a bite to eat?" You would have instead to get out—articulate—something like this: "Would you care to deflect your occlusal surfaces and stimulate your swallowing threshold with an act of deglutition?"

But the neologisms of technology, which artificially inflate our dictionaries, are similar in connotation and generally libido-poor. "The smatterer in science," Melville has a character in *White Jacket* say, "thinks that by mouthing hard words he proves that he understands hard things."[9] In this spirit everyone has become an *engineer;* the garbage collector is a sanitation engineer and Mencken even unearthed a bedding manufacturer calling himself a *sleep engineer.* This genuflection to the technocratic status quo—the golden calf of itself—reached such a point that in 1935 the National Society of Professional Engineers tried to get American railroads to call their locomotive engineers *enginemen!*

[8] *Glossary of Prosthodontic Terms,* Second Edition, compiled by the Nomenclature Committee of the Academy of Denture Prosthetics, St. Louis, Mo.: C. V. Mosby Co., 1964.

[9] Cf., also, the digression concerning *euthanasia* between the Surgeon and the Purser, forming Section 27 of Melville's *Billy Budd.*

This, then, is technology admiring itself in a mirror; for the way in which a society tells its lies is, of course, highly indicative. The effect of continuous technological euphemism is to make everything foggily similar, and in the end to work against individuality and eccentricity. The Latinate cover-up is particularly pervasive, but since it is less understood than the term for which it stands, it moves everything further from reality and truth. You can tell a man he is suffering from *agrypnia, cephalalgia, cholelithiasis,* and *pyrexia* and the immediate connotations might be somewhat similar; the words require translation and do not suggest the variety of complaints they stand for (insomnia, headache, gallstones, fever).

Just so when we redesignate *napalm* as *incendigel,* or call an *atomic bomb* a *nuclear device.* Such Pentagonese is concealing reality not for our interest but against our interest. In 1966 an Oakland student paraded with a placard demanding the outlawing of such terms as *defoliation* and *mega-deaths.*[10] (The term *classified* has come to be Pentagonese for *high-level blunder.*) The nicety of being anointed with *incendigel* rather than *napalm* must seem to an Asiatic peasant the luxury of a very rich society, indeed.[11] He has still been burnt raw by gelled gasoline fluid.

Or is it, possibly, against semantic insanity itself that the Berkeley Free Speech Movement was fundamentally protesting? "Radioactivity would damage American genes, and genetic damage might continue for up to forty generations," writes Herman Kahn of an initial thermonuclear attack in which America is conceived of as losing sixty million lives, but this is a far cry from *annihilation.* The evidence is overabundant. In a spirit of despair the layman exceeds the scientist. Since language cannot exist outside itself, since man alone is

[10] Read in this connection Lieutenant-General E. L. M. Burns, D.S.O., *Mega-Murder,* London, Harrap, 1966.

[11] When Morihiro Matsuda, a Japanese businessman, placed an ad for peace in *The Times* (London) recently, the readership was informed that "Some of the language was also delicately altered to suit the style of *The Times.* There were some refinements in translation too: 'poison gas' became 'herbicide'. . . ."

not principally a sign of something else, the consciousness of those who understand language, or the wisdom of words, contains the future, like the Trobriand magician's spells.

The most grotesque caricatures of technology, imagined by H. G. Wells in the nineties,[12] are daily coming to pass. Art Buchwald's parodies get enacted almost before they are written.[13] An ex-movie star governs the nation's most populous state, while Shirley Temple is at the U.N. We live *Dr. Strangelove* a few years after it has been tumbling us in the aisles as a ludicrous exaggeration.[14] Neil Postman invents a parodistic list of the semantics of extermination (*filteration, thermalicide,* etc.) only to find such Pentagonese as *counterforce deterrence* soon surpassing such coinages. It is significant that some of the first "democratic" critics of the arcane Johnson Administration were writers, word-handlers, like Arthur Miller and Norman Mailer. "New experiments in escalation are first denied," writes Arthur Schlesinger, Jr., "then disowned, then discounted and finally undertaken." As

---

[12] Wells's *When the Sleeper Wakes,* written during the winter of 1897–98, contains television, high-speed elevators, Boeing 747's, and a populace entranced and enslaved by technological wonders, on one hand, while, on the other, the constant threat of "the yellow peril" keeps them behind their government. Bernard Bergonzi's *The Early H. G. Wells* shows that the errand of most of Wells's science fiction was libertarian; thus, the idea of invasion by Martians was to ask Englishmen of the time what it might be like to be on the receiving end of colonization.

[13] "Every time we fire our flamethrowers," says a mythical Art Buchwald sergeant, "we are renewing our pledge to fight oppression, poverty, and disease in Southeast Asia." (New York *Herald Tribune,* February 22, 1966) Less moderate remarks were made on the Senate floor at the same time. Or compare the following, from an "open letter" to President Johnson from commentator Richard Tregaskis: "There is a problem of demonstrating the reality of our power to all of Asia. My view is that one or two hydrogen bombs can do the job with the least risk of life to our forces and the maximum effect on our future in Asia. . . . I propose it as establishing maximum effect and gaining great respect for the United States, to end the war and demonstrate not only our great strength but our respect for human rights." (New York *Herald Tribune,* Paris edition, August 31, 1966)

[14] Joyce knew that sensitivity to words involved the future and used to joke about his power of prophecy. In the "Circe" episode of *Ulysses* Bloom has a wild assimilation fantasy of being made Lord Mayor of Dublin. A few years ago, just after I had watched this passage lampooned by Zero Mostel on the stage as absurd impossibility (*Ulysses in Nighttown*), Dublin elected a Jewish Mayor.

nature rushes after art we are reminded of Dickens' Hannibal Chollop, killing for freedom. "KILL A COMMIE FOR CHRIST" was a phrase coined for a parody button; but it backfired when superpatriots carried just such placards solemnly behind effigies of the Virgin in a New York march in 1967.

Language is a Janus and will revenge itself on those who abuse it. "Twenty years' worth of Americans were taught that to lie was the highest morality," wrote Andrew Kopkind in *The New Statesman* for February 24, 1967. Today we can push Orwell's observations a stage further. If you spell it backward, it spells Nature's; or, in LBJ's similarly tail-clutching formulation, "We will continue fighting in Vietnam until the violence stops." Humpty Dumpty's question about words was what the French call *exact*—"which is to be the master—that's all." When we come to the euphemisms of contemporary war politics, when we read of *incendigel* and *megadeaths,* we remember Durkheim's warning in *Les Formes élémentaires de la vie religieuse:* "One comes to the remarkable conclusion that *images of the totem-creature are more sacred than the totem-creature itself."* One recalls that MacArthur would not lower a flag from an American position in the Pacific although that flag, which was being used as a marker by raiding Japanese planes, was costing many lives daily. This is Swift's Academy of Lagado in reverse.

And it is here that we may extrapolate Orwell somewhat. The essence of what I can only call the word-world system is a kind of language feedback. Contemporary politicians are frequently their own most enchanted listeners. Mussolini is said fatally to have taken his own words for reality, while De Gaulle has remarked, *"Quand je veux savoir ce que pense la France, je m'interroge."* Feedback implies a necessary reciprocity of message-bearing, that there should be a listener as well as a speaker. Proudhon has been called a great communications analyst; if so, it is in the sense of a cyberneticist *avant le jour,* realizing that arguments must be two-way affairs. Feedback is the basis of much "black" humor, of the effects of writers like Terry Southern and that astute semanticist Joseph Heller. It furnishes much of the pabulum for *Mad Magazine* and *The Realist.*

Our political *argot,* or language pollution, however, denies a future by its nature. It demands to be translated, but cannot be translated. Our language cannot contain the horror of our actions without leaving the rails altogether. Indeed, Pentagonese is an insulating attempt to create *another* form of language. The Vietnamese Thanh Lang is right: to usurp literature, literary techniques, in order simply and solely to deceive is the deepest form of treachery against man. To repeat over and over "COCA-COLA REFRESHES YOU BEST" is inaugurative of no possibility since the proposition is not real, it is synthetic, and meaning collapses.

Someone like Thanh Lang is surely thinking of, or more in harmony with, the sacredness of words as a necessity of any social order. Word-wisdom is a *functional* necessity. Reading Malinowski on magic, qualified as he must be now by Lévi-Strauss, one cannot but be touched by the deep sense of conscience embodied in the Trobriand magician. Before he can utter magic words at all he must be in the right matrilineal lineage, he must submit to the rigorous taboos of office, inspire constant hope and confidence in those for whom he works, stimulate them to creative effort, and eventually pass on his word-wisdom to a chosen successor. This act of moral integration is a parable of the true function of speech, and Thanh Lang describes the same original reverence for the word-user among the Vietnamese people. It is this language covenant that is broken by Western political utterance.

This is more than a mere cultural loss. It is actually a matter of sanity.[15] Used as they have been in the past decade, words like *democracy* and *freedom* end up as no more or less significant than so many street cries, or the sounds of engines. (It was Stephen Dedalus who called God "A shout in the street.") Perhaps, finally, it is the French New Novel—of Robbe-Grillet, Butor, Sarraute—that shows us what happens if man has no being beyond that of phenomenon. He is simply there, in Heidegger's First Law. And lest we dismiss the New Novel as yet another artistic exaggeration, let me point out

---

[15] MANIAC is an acronym for a weather-prediction computing device, perfected by Dr. John von Neumann—*M*athematical *A*nalyzer, *N*umerical *I*ntegrator *A*nd *C*omputer.

that in a new book, *Moment in the Sun* by Robert and Leona Rienow, we learn of an official report that has discarded the calculation of population density based on people per square mile, in favor of automobiles—"The crucial figure for United States planning is now density of cars." Man is *de trop* at last.

Orwell was right. The language of politics, the language of high abstraction, is that of robots. (Lévi-Strauss has shown the astonishing sophistication of the so-called "savage mind," which particularizes constantly.) A world of things exculpates man from being human, and we can talk like Herman Kahn. As in Faulkner's *The Sound and the Fury,* as in Sartre's *La Nausée,* or Robbe-Grillet's "fiction," time is dislocated only by space, and shapes assume their own meanings or, rather, nonmeanings.

But we observe that the protagonists of all these dramas set in a permanent present are psychotic, or—at best—highly disturbed. Sartre's Roquentin, so often misunderstood, pleads at the end for a universe with meaning, i.e., with a future. For the terminus of such existential thought is a semantic warning: if the human condition is simply to be *there,* we shan't be here much longer. "My rifle, without me, is useless. Without my rifle, I am useless. . . . My rifle is human, even as I. . . ." [16] This is not from a parody of Robbe-Grillet, but from a marine handbook.

This, then, is the nature of our nightmare, the language of politics in America. In a sense it is to be physically destroyed by language, as was Cocteau's hero Orphée. Teachers like Socrates and Gautama and Jesus preached a proper use of words because they respected the sense of harmony symbolism presented. Language is a DEW, or Distant Early Warning system. "Destroy language," the German poet Christian Morgenstern quotes Master Ekkehart as saying, "and, with it, all things and concepts. The rest is silence." Or, as the Everyday English series rewrites the Shakespearean summary, "Death now closes my utterance." So long, then, sweet elected official.

[16] United States Marine Corps, Parris Island Yearbook, 1966.

On Life Imitating Art

One of these passages is from *Catch-22:*

Morgan: He [Levy] never made you disloyal, did he?

Witness: No.

Morgan: He never made you disaffect, did he?

Witness: What does disaffect mean?

Morgan: I don't know. [Much laughter.]

Brown: Mr. Morgan, if you don't know the questions, don't ask 'em.

Morgan: I don't know the meaning of the word disaffection.

Brown: Well, do not use it in questions then.

Morgan: May I have instructions from the court then as to the meaning of the word?

Brown: You should have asked for it before you asked the question.

Morgan: I asked for a ruling . . . the other day.

Brown: . . . You should have asked me some time ago.

Morgan: I asked you . . . the other day.

Brown: It's not a proper legal proceeding to pose questions and then come back with a quick retort that you don't know the meaning of the words you used in your question.

" 'Just what the hell did you mean, you bastard, when you said we couldn't punish you?' " said the corporal who could take shorthand, reading from his steno pad.

"All right," said the colonel. "Just what the hell *did* you mean?"

"I didn't say you couldn't punish me, sir."

"When?" asked the colonel.

"When what, sir?"

"Now you're asking me questions again."

"I'm sorry, sir. I'm afraid I don't understand your question."

"When didn't you say we couldn't punish you? Don't you understand my question?"

"No, sir. I don't understand."

"You've just told us that. Now suppose you answer my question."

"But how can I answer it?"

"That's another question you're asking me."

"I'm sorry, sir. But I don't know how to answer it. I never said you couldn't punish me."

Morgan: The witness said he didn't know. . . . Colonel, I'm trying to get from you . . . the legal definition of disaffection. [This in the third week of the trial.]

Brown: You don't need it at this time. . . . I told you I'd give you a legal definition . . . at the end of the trial.

Morgan: . . . If I don't know the definition I don't know how to proceed.

Brown: Certainly as a lawyer you can reach that [a working definition] through questions.

Morgan: I don't think I can, Colonel.

Brown: If you can't then maybe you should withdraw from the case.[1]

"Now you're telling us when you did say it. I'm asking you to tell us when you didn't say it."

Clevinger took a deep breath. "I always didn't say you couldn't punish me, sir."

"That's much better, Mr. Clevinger, even though it is a barefaced lie. Last night in the latrine. Didn't you whisper that we couldn't punish you to that other dirty son of a bitch we don't like? What's his name?"

"Yossarian, sir," Lieutenant Scheisskopf said.

"Yes, Yossarian. That's right. Yossarian. Yossarian? Is that his name? Yossarian? What the hell kind of a name is Yossarian?"

Lieutenant Scheisskopf had the facts at his finger tips. "It's Yossarian's name, sir," he explained.

"Yes, I suppose it is. Didn't you whisper to Yossarian that we couldn't punish you?"

"Oh, no sir. I whispered to him that you couldn't find me guilty—"

"I may be stupid," interrupted the colonel, "but the distinction escapes me. I guess I *am* pretty stupid, because the distinction escapes me."[2]

[1]Transcript of the trial of Captain Howard Levy, quoted in the *New Republic,* June 17, 1967.

[2]From the novel *Catch-22* by Joseph Heller, Simon & Schuster, Inc., 1961.

The Language of Pledges

American Pledge of Allegiance

I pledge allegiance to the flag of the United States of America, and to the Republic for which it stands, one Nation, under God, indivisible, with Liberty and Justice for all.

Nazi S.S. Oath

Do you swear, like your forefathers, the knights of Holy German Empires, always to help those other Germans who are your brothers? Fearlessly to defend women and children? To be ready to help others in misfortune? To dedicate yourselves completely to the ideal of the German cause? Do you swear, in all circumstances and unto death, to be faithful to the oath you have sworn to your leaders, to your country, and to our Führer Adolf Hitler?

The Rifleman's Creed [1]

This is my rifle. There are many like it, but this one is mine.

My rifle is my best friend. It is my life. I must master it as I master my life.

My rifle, without me, is useless. Without my rifle, I am useless. I must fire my rifle true. I must shoot straighter than my enemy who is trying to kill me. I must shoot him before he shoots me. I will. . . .

My rifle and myself know that what counts in this war is not the rounds we fire, the noise of our burst, nor the smoke we make. We know that it is the hits that count. We will hit. . . .

[1] United States Marine Corps, Parris Island,.1966.

My rifle is human, even as I, because it is my life. Thus, I will learn it as a brother. I will learn its weaknesses, its strengths, its parts, its accessories, its sights, and its barrel. I will keep my rifle clean and ready, even as I am clean and ready. We will become part of each other.

We will. . . .

Before God I swear this creed. My rifle and myself are the defenders of my country. We are the masters of our enemy. We are the saviors of my life.

So be it, until victory is America's and there is no enemy, but Peace!

The Language of the New Politics

Pete Hamill

The pox that was 1968 is behind us, the bodies have finally
gone cold, and the New Year looms, virginal and gray. If 1969
is anything like its predecessor, we might as well just cut our
throats right now. But even with Nixon and Lodge and Hickel
and the other members of the Lawrence Welk audience who
shall govern us, there still remains some hope of survival. The
big problems might be out of our hands for four years, but
it does seem to me that on smaller matters we might have
some chance of straightening ourselves out. The following are
some suggested beginnings.

1. *An absolute cleaning up of the language.* I mean that
all of us should try to use the American language with greater
accuracy and precision. For example, in the way we talk about
race. A black racist should be called a black racist. If George
Wallace is a white racist, then Rap Brown is a black racist.
Personally, I would like to see that blurry noun "militant"
eliminated from the language. But if rewrite men continue
to use it, then it should be used across the board. If a black
yahoo like Sonny Carson can be described as a militant, then
we should also use the word to describe white yahoos like
Rosemary Gunning, Vito Battista, and Albert Shanker.

It would also help if we reduced or eliminated those phrases
which no longer have even general meaning: "groovy," "im-
perialists," "up tight," "white power structure," "piece of the
action," "pig" (as applied to all enemies, especially cops),
"participatory democracy," "Uncle Tom," "guerrilla" (followed by words like theatre, politics, journalism, painting,
etc.), "soul" (followed by food, music, brother, etc., or used
alone to connote some exalted sense of self missing in
others), "honky," "community control" (as a slab of letters
on a page, without elaboration). I realize that this would
make it almost impossible for some citizens to talk, but perhaps we would then be forced to talk with some precision

about what is happening to us. If the years of Johnson, Rostow, and Rusk have taught us anything, it is the viciousness of the sloppy use of language.

2. *Liberals in general, and intellectuals in particular, should cease functioning as excuse-makers for people who hate them.* If Rap Brown calls me a honky or a racist bastard, I have no obligation to make excuses for him; my only obligation is to laugh at him, or to belt him. I certainly have no obligation to say: yeah, Rap, oh you're beautiful, Rap, oh please lash me again, Rap, baby, give it to me some more while I make out the check. The liberals who put up with this sort of racist crap are masochist jellyfish. I realize that Rap Brown is somewhat passé, but I use him as a symbol because I've seen him work: making brave speeches about burning everything down, then disappearing behind his bodyguards while other people are beaten, kicked, arrested, or shot. The Rap Browns hate liberals because they see the liberals they bleat to (for a fee) collapse before Afros and shades faster than a French army collapses before the sight of guns. The Rap Browns have changed numbers of otherwise decent men into people who hate the sight of Negroes; the Browns gloat about this as evidence that all whites are secret racist dogs, and the liberals spend their time agreeing, and excusing Brown's filthy manners by rolling out all the history of the black man in America. The day the Rap Browns get black men into the Ironworkers Union, instead of into the cemetery, then we can believe in their sincerity about their brothers.

3. *As a footnote to the above, it should be made clear that criticism of blacks is not automatically racist.* Criticism equals racism is a beautiful piece of propaganda put forth by people who deserve to be criticized, and has paralyzed us for years. I can understand to some extent why blacks won't criticize other blacks, at least before whites (although there is no white equivalent of "Uncle Tom," and no whites have spoken as much filth about people like Bayard Rustin as blacks have). Let us grant for argument's sake that in revolutions there is some need for a united front. Still, if a black man is caught stealing from the poverty program, then he is breaking the law and should be put in the slam. To construct elaborate

theories about how the white man's law should not apply to his colonial subjects and how the black man has the right to steal or rob because his great-grandfather was stolen from Africa and robbed of his freedom and his manhood—that is sophistry. The district attorney should not be called a racist because he arrests a thief or an embezzler. If Albert Shanker breaks the law (as he clearly did), he should be put in jail; the prosecutor should not be open to a charge of anti-semitism. A thief is a thief; a lawbreaker is a lawbreaker.

Incidentally, the paranoia about "the white press" should really be described as that: paranoia. There are no conspiracies on newspapers to portray black men as raving maniacs, rapists, killers, dummies, or thieves. Paul Sann of the *Post* does not call Mike O'Neill at the *News* and Abe Rosenthal at the *Times* and set that day's line against the blacks. There are some serious inadequacies in the way race is covered, but they are the same inadequacies involved in covering everything else (crisis reporting, lack of depth and nuance, sheer dumbness, the fact that many editors don't even live in the city they purport to be covering). To stage a demonstration and then start beating the bejesus out of the people who come to cover the demonstration (most of whom are favorably disposed to your position) is not only paranoia, but stupidity.

4. *Stop the hypocrisy on inter-racial sex.* One of the great mysteries is why black women don't blow the whistle on some of their black brothers. Everyone in the Village knows this scene: the black cat sitting in the Village bar, a copy of *Liberation* in his pocket, wearing Afro and shades, practicing his best surly look, nursing a warm beer, and waiting for the first guilt-ridden white chick to tumble in the door. It doesn't matter that the girl is the ugliest white broad since Ilse Koch, or that she is sodden with whiskey, or has a bad case of the crabs. That particular black stud doesn't care. What matters is that she's white.

So, after seven or eight minutes of love talk ("white bitch," etc.), he takes her off and balls her badly on a 6th Street rooftop, and then comes back, muttering about the revolution, and has the nerve to threaten the lives of any black chicks he sees with white men. His manhood reinforced, he goes home, sleeps the sleep of the just, and spends the following morning writing an essay about black pride. Jesus. If blacks or whites have to take guys like this seriously, then we had better start erecting statues to Vincent Impelliterri, Richard Speck, and Simon Legree. They've all had an equally elevating effect on America.

5. *We should finally admit that no serious change in this country will ever be effected through Ossholism.* Abbie Hoffman and Jerry Rubin and the Yippie kids who hang around them can be funny at times, and brave. But basically they are ossholes. I cherish them for walking into HUAC meetings in costumes out of "Drums along the Mohawk." But HUAC is an easy enemy; confronting the late Joe Pool is just not the same as taking over General Motors or Litton Industries, or destroying the welfare system. The Yippies are tap-dancers and Ossholism is therapy, not politics. You don't become a revolutionary by saying you are a revolutionary, and you don't storm the Moncada Barracks with your brains blown apart on drugs.

6. *We should make some small start toward relieving the paranoia of the cops.* God knows, I have plenty of reason to believe that a lot of cops are slightly bughouse, and addled by racism and petty bigotry. But someone has to prove to me that you change them by calling them "pig" or by shooting random members of the force in the back from ambush. Cops, after all, are working-class people; they want to be respectable and their ideas about respectability are about 40 years out of date. But if you despise a cop because his hair is short, you cannot expect him to love you when yours is long. I've met cops who are decent, many who are brave, many who are not brutal sadists. They have rotten jobs, but we hired them. And let's face it: we need them. Anyone who thinks that we could survive very long in New York without cops is an innocent. I realize that I sound like Norman Frank; but the fact remains that this is a violent, brutal city, and until the golden day when really basic change is effected in the society, it will remain brutal and violent. You don't start making basic change by eliminating people on the periphery, like the cops.

I don't think we have to start putting statues of cops on

every third corner. But we could pay the cop a decent salary. We could pay him a bonus if he gets a college education (a lot of the worst cops are just ignorant). We could give the cop a sabbatical every six years or so, with pay, so he could walk around the world for a year without a gun on his hip (why schoolteachers should get sabbaticals and cops or firemen shouldn't is one of those abiding mysteries best left to some genius like Jacques Barzun). But perhaps we could begin by just once in a while saying good morning to a cop. Just for the hell of it. Just to recognize that we see him as a subject, not an object, a human being, not a uniform, a man, not a pig. (Of course, if he is a member of TPF, you might get locked up; but until the TPF is finally abolished, it's worth a shot.)

7. *We should immediately do everything possible to pass a new Lyons law.* Under the old Lyons law, which was repealed some years back, city employees had to live within the city limits. When the law was repealed, the city employees fled to the suburbs, and the result has been near-disaster. If a cop wants to be a cop and live in Oyster Bay, that's perfectly all right; just let him join the Oyster Bay PD. But if he wants to be a cop in New York City, then, by God he had better live in New York City. No one should have the right to affect the lives of people in a community in which he does not live; at present, large numbers of New York cops are functioning like Spain's Guardia Civil. They are what Charles Monaghan describes as "Hessians," taking the money, without the responsibility of paying taxes, improving the city, sharing its pain and its secrets. Anyone who lives with the barbecue-in-the-backyard life style just can't begin to understand 112th Street, the hippies, blacks, or anything else we're made of. And there is something terribly wrong when someone like Albert Shanker can disrupt our city when he doesn't even live here; he should have no more right to close our schools than he has to affect the foreign policy of Canada. The same goes for Rhody McCoy, who lives on Long Island. If they are truly concerned about our schools, let them live among us. Otherwise, to hell with them. (Insular? Sure. But if we keep exporting the middle class, then we're doomed.)

8. *We should stop cheering the Romantic Revolutionaries*

every time they call for blood. At Columbia, and in a few other places, SDS did a good job of exposing the smugness and hypocrisy (not to mention the corruption) of the people who run our institutions. But we part company on the issue of spilled blood. Talk of heading for the Adirondacks with machine guns is romantic nonsense at best, and Minuteman lunacy at worst; this is just not Cuba, or Bolivia, or Vietnam.

I remember one brave revolutionary in Chicago, who wanted to broadcast a tape recording from a loudspeaker on a high floor of the Chicago Hilton. The tape would tell the kids in Grant Park that the revolutionary was in the hotel, that they should storm the place and join him. Naturally, the kids would have been slaughtered by Daley's thugs and the National Guard. Naturally, that is what the revolutionary wanted. Naturally, he had no plans to really be in the hotel. I suppose that was a pretty clever revolutionary tactic. (The plan was never put in effect; too many objections from softies.) But personally I'm tired of the sight of blood. I've seen enough blood in the past few years to last me a lifetime; some of the blood I saw last year ran right through America, and the wounds haven't stopped hemorrhaging. For a year we could do without the sight of blood; it would be even better if "intellectuals" would cease being enthralled at the prospect of seeing it spilled.

If I seem to have spent more time here talking about the sins of the left rather than the right, it is because the left these days seems more riddled with sloppiness, intellectual arrogance, cant, and self-deception than the right. It's easy to laugh at the right, because their shibboleths are so clumsily transparent. But the cliches of the left are more sinister, because the left should be the best hope for this country. If its basic emotions are hate and contempt, then it will get nowhere. (Consider the posture of Mr. Clean, Eugene McCarthy, so blinded by hatred for the Kennedys that he found it an easy matter to vote for Russell Long in the contest for Senate majority whip.) Above all it should be the duty of the left to talk straight, without clotting its rhetoric with gooey slabs of prose glop, and without accepting every example of paranoid rubbish as revealed truth.

The Language of Bureaucracy

Henry A. Barnes

The word *bureau* has grown in significance for me over the past half century. Its earliest meaning was a chest of drawers for the bedroom, intended for the storage of personal gear unsuited to hanging in a closet or hiding under a bed.

Family ground rules demanded that the lower drawers of a bureau be maintained in reasonably orderly array, but tradition permitted the top drawer to be reserved for clutter. The top drawer was a catchall for baseball cards, pencil stubs, watch fobs, unmated shoestrings, 23-skiddoo buttons, and similar miscellany.

Unaware as I was of any other kind of bureau, I was, nevertheless, learning many useful facts for my later years spent among the bureaus of public life. Early experience taught me that a bureau requires constant supervision lest it become a mare's-nest of disorder. Another lesson fixed in memory is the knowledge that the periodic reorganizing of a bureau can become a refuge from reality, a dawdler's delight which provides the aimless with endless hours of seemingly productive endeavor.

An early organizing technique was to divide the bureau into divisions. This might be accomplished in the lower drawers, but never in the top drawer. The attempt was usually made with the aid of partitions consisting of discarded cigar and candy boxes. The boxes were seldom suitable for the job, being selected to fit the space rather than the purpose. The result resembled the printed forms of modern bureaucracy—small boxes for long items and big boxes for short items.

Bureaucrat and *bureaucracy* were words I had never heard. I probably would have associated them with *aristocrat* and *aristocracy,* and concluded that a bureaucrat was a boy who didn't have to share a bureau with his brother. A bureaucracy would, no doubt, have been a fanciful state in which such affluent isolation prevailed.

Since those days of innocence, I have learned that many words have more than one meaning—*bureau* among them. Many such words have been directed my way—*bureaucrat* among them. These confrontations lose their jolt with time, but I am still dismayed when anyone, in evident compliment, refers to me as a "top-drawer bureaucrat."

Bureaucracy generally carries the connotation of an impersonal governmental agency insulated alike from reality and responsibility by layers of red tape. It is in this context that I intend to pursue the subject of the language of bureaucracy. It would be unrealistic, however, to ignore the fact that bureaucracy arises also in private enterprise, and its language is spoken wherever an organization becomes so large and complex and detached that it loses the common urge to communicate in the common tongue with others.

The grating voice of bureaucracy's jargon may be heard in any organization, public or private, which feels itself free of the need to share a bureau with its brothers.

When the profits of industry go down, the towers of bureaucratic babel go up. I have read corporation reports which were based on the assumption that the stockholder has at his disposal as many lawyers, accountants, and word-splitters as the firm itself. I have heard executives from the "private sector of the economy" spatter audiences with such eloquent nonsense as: "This is a novel innovation of such dimension, scope, and proportion that, without a certain doubt, it is a boon and benefit not only to all mankind but to every customer, employee, and stockholder of this enterprise."

While much of the language of bureaucracy defies precise decipherment, it will be found that about 50 percent of the spoken language, including the foregoing example, consists of variations of a single sentence—"Keep your eye on the girl with the pretty legs while I prepare to pull another rabbit out of the hat."

At this point it may be to my advantage to state that the examples of the language of bureaucracy presented here have been subjected to considerable paraphrasing to protect the guilty.

One very useful method of translating the spoken language of bureaucracy is to commit it to print. In the following example, truth crushed to earth in a bureaucrat's dictation rose again, inadvertently, in his secretary's typing.

> *Example:*
> This little-publicized program has been endorsed by a hundred-odd officials.
> *Translation:*
> This little, publicized program has been endorsed by a hundred odd officials.

It will be noted that the hidden meaning of the dictated version was revealed in the typing by simple revision of punctuation. One who has worked for an appreciable time in areas where the jargon of bureaucracy prevails learns other simple translation devices. For instance, all expressions of confidence should be interpreted as evidences of doubt. A simple way to remember this rule is to bear in mind the true significance of *confidence man.*

As indicated below, a little practice with simple words and phrases of assurance and conviction will enable the student to move quickly to more complex sentences.

> *Example:*
> Doubtless
> *Translation:*
> Unverified

> *Example:*
> Interesting fact
> *Translation:*
> Drivel

> *Example:*
> Universally recognized principle
> *Translation:*
> A risky proposition

Example:
> We are assigning major priority to the early completion of the preliminary stages of the program.

Translation:
> With any luck we can forget the matter completely.

It must not, however, be assumed that translations may always be accomplished so readily. Since the technique of the bureaucrat is to pour more words than light on his subject, all surplus words must be deleted before any translation can be attempted. To fully understand this principle, one must remember that an important rule of the language of bureaucracy requires, wherever possible, the use of two or more difficult words selected by sound, rather than one simple word chosen for meaning.

Example:
> The respondent correspondent gave expression to the unqualified opinion that the subject missive was anterior to his facile comprehension.

Translation:
> He replied that he didn't understand our letter.

The thought presents itself here that English grammarians can be rather bureaucratic in their insistence on conformity. Some of the most interesting addresses I have heard have been among the least grammatical. But this is a subject of a different discussion.

The language of bureaucracy is essentially a professional jargon. Like other professional jargons it lends itself to exclusiveness, defensiveness, and laziness. A thorough study of this or any other private language would require psychological and sociological analyses of the structure, functions, conditions, and mentality which created the desire for a special lingo. Two difficulties to this approach present themselves—the space limitations of this article, and the author's inability to under-stand the professional jargons of the psychologists and sociolo-gists. So without extensive examination of the motivational aspects, let us consider a few of the factors bearing on the formation of the private bureaucratic jargon.

Bureaucracy is often called "The System." This is, perhaps, some small recognition of the fact that a bureaucracy has its origin in the good intention of achieving systematic operation. All "inside" languages begin with a group's desire to foster efficiency. It is only when the group loses or discards its initial motivation to serve the general public that the "outside" language falls into discard. The "inside" tongue now develops in direct proportion to the group's new inclination to isolate itself and deceive or confuse outsiders.

Contrary to popular belief, the language of bureaucracy is not essential to success in public life. The names of Adlai Stevenson and Robert Moses come readily to mind as ex-amples of public figures who have used the common English language with grace, skill, and effectiveness.

Such men have no need for the protective cover of an "inside" language. The jargon of bureaucracy developed from the needs of lesser men to make their lives easier, shield their shortcomings, or cover the drabness of their operations with some tawdry gloss.

The desire to make life easier fosters the growth of routine phrasing to fit routine situations. Clichés replace original thought. Perfunctory phrases chill response. Dullness is mis-taken for dignity. Ready-made replies are stockpiled to handle recurring questions.

The form letter is, perhaps, the most exasperating evidence of this tendency. From the standpoint of the bureaucrat, the form letter is a survival kit on the barren mountain of corre-spondence. To the citizen with a unique problem, the form letter is an abomination.

Originating as bureaucracy's fence against avalanches of official correspondence, the form letter becomes in time a despotic protector against work and worry. The periodic at-tempts of committees to revise form letters or to make them applicable to new types of correspondence often succeed only in spreading the same old ineffective unction more thinly over additional wounds. The time-saving device now becomes a time-wasting irritant as bureaucracy vainly attempts to channel the warm pulsings of civic life into cold classifications like so many columns of want ads.

Heavy reliance on ready-made replies eventually reduces bureaucracy's ability to express itself clearly when a tailor-made reply is required. New constructions are introduced into its language to mask its deficiencies. Emphasis is sought by stacking superlative on superlative. Unpleasant facts are hidden behind screens of flamboyant words. Tautology impedes meaning. The plague of -*ants*—pursu*ant,* cogniz*ant,* convers*ant,* result*ant*—is turned loose. Ideas are lost in the maze of complex sentences. A shortage of meaning develops in direct proportion to the surplus of words.

Just as bureaucracy feeds on carbon copies, its language fattens on the repetition of words. Adjectives must always be accompanied by their identical twins and all known relatives. To a bureaucrat, the United States is not merely a big country, it is a huge, vast, and spacious nation. Certain words in the bureaucrat's vocabulary may not decently appear in public without their chaperons. The story is told of an agency which could not prepare a notice for an employees' social because it was impossible to separate *social* from *political* and *economic* in an official document.

Some of the long and legalistic phrasing in the language of bureaucracy results from the public servant's duty to protect the public interest. If any fault attaches to it, the special jargon of the law should be held accountable. Contracts are prime examples. In a contract which I signed for my department recently was a sentence composed of 279 words. This lengthy sentence merely stated that the contractor could lose his contracts and be barred from further bidding if he refused to testify in any legal proceedings. Although the thought can be stated here in a couple of dozen words, this simple version would be powerless to withstand the attacks of an astute attorney. Loophole-stuffing of this kind accounts for a considerable amount of the padding in official correspondence.

In my years in public service, I have noted a gradual improvement in the language of bureaucracy as used externally. Internally, however, where committee reports rise like magnificent tombstones over the remains of the English language, improvements have been scarce.

Much of the fault lies in bureaucracy's passion for prepackaged decisions—advance planning to remove all possibility of personal judgment and initiative. Although as an individual man is seldom gifted with prophetic vision, as a member of a committee he feels himself equal to any future emergency. With his co-oracles, he finds no difficulty in producing such dogma as this:

PROCEDURES, EMERGENCY
Instruction #20973 A-3 (1964)
Section 794—Attack, Atomic

In the possible event of an atomic attack, the senior administrative officer in effective attendance (see Personnel Order 000.06) shall proceed in strict compliance and accordance with applicable provisions of General Circular #87 (1951), paragraphs 843 to 976 as amended by General Circular #103 (1952), paragraphs 237 to 743 and 821 to 934.

Due care must be exercised to comply completely and fully with Office Procedure Manual #1 (1901) Section F-103 (Catastrophes, major) Section V-19 (Absence, excused) and Section W-47 (Routines, timecards).

Reference may profitably be made to Emergency Procedures—Instruction #45678 R-7 (1964) under the subsequently following headings:

Cave-in, roof (Section 279)
Pipes, steam, broken (Section 293)
Pipes, water, broken, hot (Section 483-A)
Pipes, water, broken, cold (Section 483-J)
Elevators, service, none (Section 791)
Stairways, use of (Section 904)

Reports will be made in quadruplicate to the executive office on Forms #3290R (1904), #5280 (1907) and 7654321-G (1960). Separate forms will be completed for each employee concerned. Filing of reports is mandatory and required during the work day on which emergency occurs.

NOTE: The above enumeration of forms is not to be

construed or interpreted to excuse the senior administrative officer from using all other appropriate forms applicable to the circumstance obtaining.

IMPORTANT: No disbursements of agency funds will be permitted nor may agency vehicles be used by other than assigned personnel without prior approval in writing from the bureau head or his duly appointed representative on written request to be filed at least two (2) weeks in advance of the date upon which permission shall become operative.

Assuming that the documents, pertinent, have not been consumed in a holocaust, fiery, the officer, administrative, senior, need spend only an hour or two decoding the instructions and another few hours in preparing reports to emerge as the hero, unquestioned, of the situation.

A word might be said for the public servant who struggles daily through this jungle of bureaucratic entanglements. His pretentious phrasings are often the reflection of a dull and repetitious existence rather than a pompous personality. Frequent flowery redundancies in the language of bureaucracy are comparable to the sports writer's thesaurus-like reports. A person doomed to tell the same story daily deserves some commendation for his efforts to tell it in a new way.

All the elements for continual growth persist, but one small peril to the language of bureaucracy has begun to develop. This is a problem of bureaucracy's own making—the long evasive answer. For years this technique permitted a bureaucrat the advantage of a revolving door of words from which he could emerge on either side at his own convenience. A classic instance of its use is in the final moments of a radio or TV interview to prevent the moderator from asking the question he was saving for the final discomfiture of the bureaucrat. Moderators are now learning to counter this tactic with the long evasive question which leaves the bureaucrat only seconds to answer a query he probably doesn't understand. Thus a medium of communications with major influence on the development of language patterns begins to veer toward the language of bureaucracy. If the trend continues, bureaucracy may be forced for self-protection to return to the use of the English language.

The Price of a Square Meal

BOARD OF EDUCATION
THE CITY OF NEW YORK

110 Livingston St., Brooklyn 1, New York

Date _____ 19 _____

Name of Pupil _____   P.S. _____ Boro _____

Class _____   Room _____

Residence _____   Boro _____

Dear Sir or Madam:

Do you wish your child, as listed above, to be furnished with lunch at this school?

Yes _____ No _____

Lunches are served without cost, to those entitled to same, or sold by the week at an established price.

Do you wish to pay?   Yes _____ No _____

If you wish lunch furnished without cost, please answer questions below:

(1) Are you on Department of Welfare Assistance?   Yes _____ No _____

(2) If so, give your Case Number and check the type of public assistance you receive.

Case Number _____

Home Relief ☐   Veterans Assistance ☐

Aid to Dependent Children ☐   Foster Care ☐

(3) What is the location of the Welfare Center that handles your case?
_____

(4) If you are not on Department of Welfare Assistance, what is the total weekly family income from all sources? _____

(5) How many persons in your family, living at home, depend upon this income for support? _____

(6) What is the name and address of your employer?
_____
_____

(If you have more than one source of income, list all additional sources of income on the reverse side of this form)

PARENT'S SIGNATURE _____

Please return this form to the Principal of the School.

Very truly yours,

SUPERINTENDENT OF SCHOOLS

Based upon the information furnished by the parent or guardian on this form, I certify that the child named on this certificate is eligible for a free lunch.

_____
Signature of Principal or Person in Charge

The Language of the Liberal Arts
(Circa 1968)

From the Washington Square College (NYU) Bulletin:

To receive credit for a course, a student must be regular in his attendance and satisfactorily complete all examinations and other assignments prescribed by the instructor.

Students will receive grades according to the following scale: A (excellent); B (good); C (fair); D (work meeting only minimum requirements); F (failure). Academic averages are computed as a grade point credit ratio on a 4-point scale in which A equals 4 points; B, 3 points; C, 2 points; D, 1 point; and F, 0 points. All grades of A, B, C, D, or F earned in Washington Square College will be used in the computation of the average. This is true also of grades earned in courses taken by special permission for purposes of review, even though credit is not awarded.

A weighted average is obtained by dividing the sum of the grade points earned (0 to 4 for each credit hour) by the number of credit hours covered by the grade points. For example, a student earning a grade of B in a 4-point course and a grade of C in a 4-point course will have a total of 20 grade points (12 + 8) and a weighted average of 2.5.

The temporary grade of I (incomplete) will be reported only if a student may later earn credit for the course and has, *for good reason,* not completed a required part of the course or taken the final examination. (A student whose work up to the time of the final examination has been below passing and who is absent from the test will receive a grade of F and not I.) Grades of I reported in the fall semester must be removed by the end of the next spring semester, and such grades reported in the spring semester or in the summer must be removed by the end of the next fall semester. If a grade of I is not so removed, a terminal grade of N will be reported, and the student may no longer earn credit in the course unless he reregisters and repeats the course.

The following grades are considered to be terminal: A, B, C, D, F, N, P, S, U, and W.

The grades S (satisfactory) and U (unsatisfactory) are reported only for those required physical education, thesis consultation, and military or air science courses for which no point credit is given.

The grade W is used to report an official withdrawal from course. (*See* page 199, "Withdrawal from Courses.")

A grade of N (no credit) or F (failure) will be reported for a course in which a student has been excessively absent. (*See* pages 199–200, "Absence from Class.")

The grade of P is used instead of A, B, C, or D when a student passes a course for which he has registered on a pass-fail basis.

The Language of Censorship

James Lincoln Collier

The thing that has always fascinated me most about language is the way it can be used to conceal meanings. There are a number of devices for doing the hiding, but the easiest and most often practiced method is the substitution of Latinate words for Anglo-Saxon. For example, "profit motive" is precisely synonymous with the word "greed." Both mean the desire for wealth at the expense of anybody else, but because the words themselves fail to suggest the correspondence, most people fail to notice it. Another interesting bit of contemporary trumpery is the phrase "the people's right to know." It is exercised largely by newspaper publishers and editors in defense of their desire to publish evidence against criminal defendants which would be inadmissible in court, and means, of course, "the publisher's right to print whatever he wants." There is no need to labor the point: hunting out the hidden meaning in shibboleths is a game anybody with a rudimentary instinct for verbal analysis can play.

One area in which I have played over the years is censorship. It is, indeed, a most fascinating field in which to play because censorship involves the arraignment of language itself. It is the homage power pays to words. It is language judging language; and this fact gives the game of hidden meanings a special piquancy.

In exploring the language of censorship, especially in contemporary America, the main object is to find out what is being censored, and why. We might expect some difficulties in reaching the second objective; reaching the first we should expect to pose no real problems. As it happens, however, it is the old business of greed and the profit motive: the language in which our censorship codes are expressed works quite thoroughly to conceal what it is really all about. The camouflage is so well made, in fact, that so far as I know the meaning behind the words has never been commented upon. The unhappy truth is, however, that our native variety of censorship tells us something perfectly extraordinary about class division and the failure of democracy in our social system.

The odd thing about American censorship is that it is, ostensibly at least, nonpolitical. Over the centuries, censors have been employed by the state primarily to keep orators and pamphleteers from explaining to the people how they have been cheated, and thus bringing on revolution and such of its accoutrements as fire and the guillotine. (I assume medieval Church censorship to fall into this category.) Even today, leaving aside a half dozen European nations and two or three exceptional countries elsewhere, all world governments assume the right to suppress remarks critical of authority. Political censorship is as much a fact in France and West Germany as it is in Russia and Red China. To be sure, the Western princes are more circumspect than the Eastern in the exercise of this right, but they assume it nonetheless.

By contrast, in the United States we have actually seen published and well publicized a play which accuses a President of complicity in the assassination of his predecessor. We have heard civil-rights orators call with impunity for armed revolt, despite laws against advocating the violent overthrow of the government. We have seen peace demonstrators accuse government officials of mass murder and urge support for a country we are at war with. The truth of the matter is that there exists in the United States today a freedom of speech in political matters which is almost absolute. What would happen if the government decided that, say, the Negro revolution was really dangerous is another question; but the fact remains that at present our freedom to criticize authority is quite remarkable.

American political censorship is almost entirely concerned with what I suppose I have to call sexual materials. I think that this is reasonably evident. In recent years a number of men, including the hapless Ralph Ginzburg, publisher of *Eros,* have been convicted of distributing sexual materials, whereas nobody has been even locked up for advocating the overthrow of the government. Pamphlets and papers violently critical of the government—some of them urging its overthrow —are readily available, whereas a fairly considerable amount of printed material wholly sexual in content is suppressed every year. Clearly, the concern of American censorship is sex.

The legal code which enforces this censorship has never been worked out with any exactitude. It has been got up by teeming thousands of boards of selectmen and town councils across the nation, usually in response to the shrill cries of outraged motherhood or the grim dedicated thunder of a local priest. There is nothing in the world easier for a politician to oppose, and harder to support, than smut. As a consequence, most towns of any size, and a great many other corporate entities— villages, counties, townships and so forth—have laws prohibiting the sale of obscene material. What this means, for the most part, is that nearly every newsstand in the country lies under the gun of a local sheriff or police chief empowered to remove books and magazines from the stands at his own discretion. On top of these thousands of rules are the laws of the states, nearly all of which prohibit the distribution of obscenity. And over the state laws are Federal codes operating through the post office, which is not supposed to carry obscene material; the customs office, which is not supposed to admit it to the country; and the Interstate Commerce Commission, which is supposed to keep it from moving from state to state.

Thrown all together, this vast heap of legal language makes up a patchwork obscenity code which is irregular, often improper, and occasionally contradictory. Built largely out of words like "lascivious," "tending to corrupt," "obscene," "perverted," "filthy," and the like, it is difficult for the inexperienced to interpret. For example, you cannot define perversion until you have defined normality, and nobody, in the area of sex anyway, has been able to do that yet. One's man's filth is another man's harmless diversion.

And yet surprisingly, beneath this shapeless, watery language is a censorship code which in practice is quite consistent. It exists mainly as a consensus in the minds of the customs officials and sheriffs charged with enforcing it; and, since sheriffs and customs officials are people too, it reflects, at least roughly, what the generality of Americans think. If you ask a random sampling of small-town police chiefs to point out the obscene magazines on the rack at the corner drugstore they will choose the same titles with an astonishing consistency.

This is not mere speculation on my part. As it happens, for a number of years I worked as writer, editor, and picture editor for types of magazines which are anxious to know what small-town police chiefs will do. These are the cheesecake magazines, men's adventure magazines, confession and fan magazines, and a few others of a similar nature. Publications of this kind perpetually run along the borderline between clean and dirty. In fact, they do so deliberately. In a highly competitive business, each editor strives to include the sexiest material he can without raising the ire of those thousands of officials in towns small and large. It doesn't hurt much to get in trouble in a couple of places. However, if your magazines are removed from the racks in too many places at once, you stand to lose money on that issue. (It doesn't matter that the local officials will usually lose in the courts if you press them. The particular issue of the magazine is normally long dead by the time you win, and besides, lawsuits cost money.)

As a consequence, the people who put out these magazines have developed a very keen sense of the real pornography code buried under the loose language of the official one. They know what, as a practical matter, American obscenity law actually says. And what it says, in some respects, is quite astonishing.

Let me summarize briefly. It is generally illegal in the United States to describe in text or depict in illustrations the genitals of male or female, excrement and excretory processes, and any of the various sex acts. It is permissible to state that an act of coitus has taken place; it is also permissible to state that a homosexual act has taken place, but it is not permissible to note the type of act. It is not allowed to state that an act of incest, bestiality, or non-coital sex has occurred. And finally, it is not permitted to use any of the short words for the genitals or the sex acts.

In broad outline this is the law. There are, however, some

rather odd details woven into this law. To begin with, a magazine which costs fifty cents or more may show any part of the female body except the genitals, pubic hair, and anus; a magazine which costs less than fifty cents may show none of these, nor the rosette and nipple of the breast. There is this exception, however: a magazine priced under fifty cents may show the nipples of Asiatics and Negroid members of non-literate cultures. And then there is this further exception: any magazine with a net paid circulation of one million copies or above may reproduce illustrations of statues, and copies of paintings or other works of art in which the genitals are visible, provided that the genital area occupies less than ten percent of the area of the illustration. And another exception: reproductions of works of art or statuary depicting people in the sex act may be used in any book printed on 80-pound stock or heavier which is at least twelve inches in height and which retails for $7.50 or above.

There are a few other curiosities of this sort in our unwritten pornography law, but the above will suffice for the moment. These exceptions to the rules may seem silly, and certainly they have been broken with impunity thousands of times. Nevertheless, any publisher who breaks the law as I have outlined it risks having his material impounded; and anyone who breaks it regularly is likely to be convicted of a crime.

But why the inconsistency? Why should price or format make a thing clean or dirty? In order to find out we have to go for an answer, or the beginning of an answer, to the Supreme Court.

The Supreme Court has generally held the written, ostensible censorship code to be unconstitutional. (There is no way to rule on the *unwritten* code, because it is not "law"; therefore we have no way of knowing how the court stands on it.) Over the years the Court has consistently decided that obscenity is not protected by the First Amendment; but just as consistently it has struck down those portions of the patchwork code which have been brought before it.

The problem is one of language. What a censorship law has to do, if it is to reflect the American consensus, is to make a clear distinction between permissible erotic material like pin-up pictures, and so-called "hard-core" pornography—itself an entrancing example of word formation by unconscious metaphor. In many types of law it is possible to make quite precise distinctions between what is legal and what is illegal. The trick is to use some measure or system of abstraction outside of language—numbers in the case of much commercial law, weights in food and drug law, and so forth. In censorship, by contrast, you are using language to measure language. It is like checking the accuracy of a ruler against a mark you have measured off with the ruler: all you learn is that the ruler is as long as itself, and you knew that anyway. The language of censorship—"obscene," "pornographic," "filthy," "lascivious," and so forth—consists merely of synonyms—a handful of rulers cut from the same pattern. Obscenity, the laws have traditionally said, is illegal: but what is obscene? So the Supreme Court has struck down most laws on the grounds that the wording was too vague.

It has felt bad about doing so. It hasn't seemed to the Court fair to tell people that censorship was legal but that the empowering laws weren't. As a consequence, in a decision in what is known to censorship buffs as the Roth Case, it attempted to settle the problem once and for all.

Samuel Roth, a Polish immigrant, had spent most of his life selling erotic material through the mails and thumbing his nose at the Post Office Department, for which he had been convicted and jailed on several occasions. After his last conviction in 1956 Roth, then over sixty, appealed to the Supreme Court, and in 1957 the Court, in upholding the conviction, handed down the basic rule for obscenity which remains today the keystone holding up the whole of our censorship law. The crucial portion of the ruling says that the test of obscenity is "whether to the average person, applying contemporary community standards, the dominant theme of the material taken as a whole appeals to the prurient interest."

This was the Supreme Court's solution to the problem of separating hard-core pornography from what is generally acceptable erotica—the cheesecake magazines, certain literary classics, and much of the contemporary arts generally. The solution was ingenious. What the Court said, in essence, was that anything is obscene the bulk of which a jury of standard Americans decides is obscene. In other words, since you cannot define obscenity in language, you simply let the general run of people, through proper judicial processes, decide what they will not stand for.

But even the cleverest of men cannot make a ruler which measures itself. Once again the Court has failed to look behind its Latinate vocabulary to find out what it really has said. The troublesome phrase is "prurient interest." According to some standard desk dictionaries I have consulted, "prurient" means things like: "eagerly lustful"; "having lascivious longings"; "to itch, crave, be wanton"; and "having lustful ideas or desires." It is hard to see, therefore, how "appeals to the prurient interest" can mean anything other than "arouses sexual desire." If there is any doubt about it, try and think of something else the phrase might mean; appealing to the prurient interest either means stirring up of sexual feeling, or it means nothing at all.

And in plain fact, this is what sexual censorship has really always been about, anyway. The Supreme Court chose to conceal its meaning behind language, but in an early day, courts were not so fastidious. One 1920's court decision ruled a book permissible because it would not "excite lustful or lecherous desire." Somewhat later Judge Benjamin Greenspan let *God's Little Acre* off with the remark, "This is not a book . . . which would tend to incite lustful desires in the normal mind," and Judge Woolsey in the famous decision which let Joyce's *Ulysses* past customs said that "it would not stir the sex impulses of any person with a normal mind."

What the Supreme Court has done behind the delicate phrasing of the Roth decision, then, is something fairly silly. As a group, the American people spend millions of man-hours a day attempting to arouse the prurient interests of each other. Women doctor their exteriors to achieve this effect, teenagers buy beer for their girls to accomplish it. Mass entertainment, fashion, the advertising industry, and dozens of other institutions play upon it in order to satisfy that other interest of right-thinking people, the profit motive. Indeed, it is quite probable that the main function of the human being is the arousing of prurient interest in somebody else.

The Supreme Court, obviously, was not laboring under the delusion that it ought to stop people from wanting to have sexual intercourse. Just as obviously, however, the entire body of Anglo-Saxon sexual censorship and, to a lesser degree, all sexual censorship in the Western world, has been aimed at reducing sexual desire. There is, however, a great more to it than that, and in order to understand what that more is—and what censorship has to do with American democracy—we need to look back over a bit of history.

There is an erroneous impression generally abroad that the so-called sex revolution of the current century is a reaction to a long period of sexual repression dating back to—well, a long time ago. Western civilization, over its long history, has pendulated between periods of sexual repressiveness and relative leniency. These periods are not all of a piece, but tend to be especially lenient or especially harsh on one or another type of sexual behavior. For example, in this century in America, bestiality is treated in the courts as a minor offense, if it gets into them at all, while forcible rape often rates the death sentence. By contrast, in seventeenth-century New England the death sentence was given for bestiality, and rape was treated as a relatively minor crime. Again, in the Hebrew culture prior to the time of the prophets, homosexuality was very close to acceptable, but adultery was considered a major crime. In contemporary America, homosexuality is the far more anathematized of the two.

In any case, the modern history of sexual attitudes in the West, speaking very broadly, begins with a period of severe repression in the late medieval period, which gradually loosened as part of the attitude changes known as the Renaissance. Contrary to popular opinion, the Protestant movement was not generally repressive of (at least) coital sex, and the bonds continued to relax through most of the eighteenth century, when leniency began to border on license. Then, toward the end of the eighteenth century the pendulum began to swing back, bringing on the so-called Victorian Age, a time of considerable sexual repression. In turn this period began dying just before the twentieth century, and ended with the close of the first World War.

Like other periods of sexual repression, the Victorian Age took its own curious shape. What the Victorians were most concerned about was not any particular form of sex act, but the giving to sex any publicity whatever. It was the word, not the deed, which really worried the Victorians. A quite elaborate super-language of euphemisms was developed to cover those aspects of sex, such as pregnancy, which simply had to be talked about. Women were shrouded from head to toe, and even furniture legs were clothed in ruffles to eliminate the suggestion of sex. The short sexual words, which had been in most dictionaries for three hundred years, were dropped out. Thomas Bowdler cleaned up Shakespeare, giving his name to the language, and as early as 1818 Noah Webster expurgated the Bible, announcing that parts of it were not fit to be read in the family, or, incredibly, the pulpit.

On the other hand, Victorian sexual behavior, insofar as we know what it was, was not nearly so repressive as the intolerance of its display suggests. Under the mantle of decency there flourished a virulent prostitution, which involved debauching large numbers of the female poor. As the testimony in the Wilde case reveals, homosexuality and homosexual prostitution were tolerated at least in the upper classes. Many men who could afford it took mistresses, and, if people like Frank Harris are to be believed, relatively casual copulation was hardly rare.

The real force of Victorian prudery bore not against the sex act, but against verbalizing it. To be sure, the Victorian Age was hardly a time of great looseness in sexual behavior. Yet the general feeling was that it was not the act that mattered so much, as the appearance of it. The scandal was not the fornication, but the publicly pregnant unwed woman. The very language of Victorian social codes suggests as much: people were told to be "discreet," "circumspect," and "modest," and to "respect appearances." More than anything, what the Victorians wanted to do was to avoid stirring up people's sexual desires—their prurient interest. If people were discreet, they could do what they wanted. Oscar Wilde, it should be remembered, was ostracized by his peers not for what he did—a lot of people did that sort of thing—but for making a public scandal of it.

But Victorian censorship has one curious aspect which has not been noticed much, if at all. It was not directed at the entire population, but at two distinct classes of people. One was children, whom I will leave aside for the purposes of this essay. The other was that large group best described as the working class—what the British called the lower order.

It is easier to infer this fact than demonstrate it directly. The Anglo-Saxon upper classes that administered this censorship never admitted that it was discriminatory, if in fact they were aware of what they were really doing. However, by looking over the rulings of the court, where practical censorship law is usually made anyway, the intention of the dicta becomes quite clear. Take the key case in British and American obscenity law, *Regina v. Hicklin* in 1868. In the decision, Chief Justice Alexander Cockburn—one of those lucky accidents of nomenclature with which censorship fans are blessed—ruled, "And I think the test of obscenity is this, whether the tendency of the matter charged as obscene is to deprave and corrupt *those whose minds are open to such immoral influences,* and into whose hands a publication of this sort may fall." (My emphasis.)

The careful listener can find echoes of the Hicklin rule in obscenity decisions ever since. In 1894, for example, one judge in this country instructed a jury to determine whether the material in question "would suggest or convey lewd and lascivious thoughts to the young and inexperienced." In another case in the same decade Judge Morgan J. O'Brien, ruling on the permissibility of various literary classics, said, "There is no such evil to be feared from the sale of these rare and costly books as the imagination of many even well-disposed people might apprehend. They rank with the higher

literature, and would not be bought or appreciated by the class
of people from whom unclean publications ought to be with-
held." And as late as the 1920's a New York jurist ruled that
a play was obscene because it "might give to some minds a
lecherous swing, causing corruption of the moral tone of the
susceptible members of the audience."

In all of these rulings it is not everybody, but a certain
vaguely specified group of people that is discriminated against.
If it needs any further proving what group this is, consider
the way in which erotic materials are made available even
today. The general run of cheap, badly printed erotica is sold
furtively and is often prosecuted. On the other hand, material
which is essentially the same in subject matter, but expen-
sively printed and bound, and made available through large,
respectable bookstores, librarians, and art schools, is sold
openly, without fear of the police. It is not easy for a blue-
collar worker to get hold of a close-up picture of female
genitals, for example, but as a professional with a little money
to spend, I can order a copy of *Dickenson's Anatomy of Sex,*
a standard work which contains enough drawings of genitals
of all sorts to last an ordinarily prurient man for a lifetime.
If I want to look at pictures of any of limitless variations in
sexual activity I can get *Fuch's History of the Erotic in Art*
at the public library. If I want to read lists of four-letter words
I can consult the Heritage Press edition of Rabelais. If I want
to read sexy stories I can turn to Balzac's *Droll Stories.*

My blue-collar contemporary, however, has extremely
limited access to sexual materials of this kind. This is partly
because he can't afford to buy it, partly because he doesn't
know how to go about getting it, and partly because he has
been conditioned to shy away from the formidable institutions which stand guard over our culture.

But what is going on? Why should the Victorians create
a censorship directed primarily at a single class of people—and
why should we want to keep it going?

The key fact, one which we have largely forgotten, is that
the spoils which belong to the victors include the women as
well as the loot. In fact, there is good reason to guess that

a lot of wars are started by sexually deprived people whose prime purpose is to obtain command over a supply of women. In any case, the winners in the class struggle of modern times in the West gained not only control of the bulk of the available property, but enlarged rights to the women as well.

Eighteenth- and nineteenth-century gentlemen customarily expected to have access to girls drawn from the lower classes. They seduced them with promises, they bought them from their fathers and mothers, or they simply found them homeless on the streets and made mistresses of them. In America, this sexual exploitation of the poor began when mass immigration created a source of women willing to fill the brothels of the cities as an escape from the sweatshops.

I do not mean to claim that this sexual exploitation was organized, or justified, or even expressed. It was just that the ordinary upper-class male throughout his life got a considerable proportion of sexual activity with working-class women, one way or another: but on the other hand, the working-class male hardly ever had access to women in the class above him. Not only this: if a working-class girl was good-looking enough, or remarkable in some other respect, there was every chance that she could escape her origins and move into the upper-class social system. Through whatever combination of law, conditioning, rules felt and rules understood, fear, and passivity, the Victorian system allowed the gentry within certain limits to take their pick of lower-class women—but refused lower-class men reciprocal rights.

When a small group of people in any social system gains control of most of the wealth, as was the case in the nineteenth century in most of the West, it is going to be faced with the problem of defending its loot against the envy of the have-nots. Similarly, when such a group gets a corner on the women, it is going to be faced with an equally intense jealousy. It is no accident that the police force, with its mandate to protect private property, originated in concert with Victorian prudery.

Historically, one of the most important events in the West during the period I am speaking of was the blood bath of the French Revolution. Ruling-class opinion, which had been tending toward liberalism, reversed itself, deathly frightened by the potentiality for violence it suddenly recognized in the lower class. It is of course too much to trace Victorian sexual ideology solely to the Reign of Terror; but the fact remains that the swing toward prudery follows hard on the heels of the guillotine. In any case, it is reasonable to see the Victorian attitude as a function of the class warfare which was the chief product of the Industrial Revolution.

The winners in the class struggle after the Industrial Revolution created a constabulary to protect their property, and they created a sexual censorship to preserve their sexual spoils. They expected that the ban on erotic material would do two things. First, it would conceal from the masses what fun the classes were having. Second, it would keep from the masses material likely to inflame their sexual feelings. The Victorian authorities hardly worked this all out clearly in their heads. The censorship code was built on the half-understood feeling that "they" were dangerous, filled with sudden passions which could sweep "them" into pillage and rapine. Any good middle-class boy of my generation who lived in a town with a Polish, or Italian, or Hungarian, or whatever other working-class minority clustered at one side of town knows what the feeling is. Down there "they" get drunk a lot and fight and smash things; certainly no decent girl would be safe there.

The Victorians thus created a morality built around discretion, which anathematized envy and violence, and punished rape with death. Decent women were clothed from head to toe so that they would not arouse lascivious thoughts in the working-class people who saw them on the streets; and an iron-fisted censorship, made necessary by the first mass literacy in the history of the world, shut off sexually heating material.

There is a fascinating parellel to this complex of law and feeling in the subculture existing in the American South.

There the white winners of the class struggle have always had almost unlimited access to the women of the losing Negro; yet in reverse, the Negro male who attempts to seduce a white woman risks, even today, almost certain death. The South has not created a censorship; but its equivalent exists in the constant harping fear among whites that, given his freedom, the Negro male would range free among the white women.

In any case, it should be clear why thirty-five-cent magazines must be more circumspect than the more expensive ones. The men's adventure magazines, the confession magazines, and the rest of them are made to appeal to the people of the blue-collar class. The more expensive magazines—*Playboy* is the prime example—are aimed at a middle-class, white-collar audience. And this, of course, is not the whole of it. Television, pre-eminently *the* blue-collar medium, as listener polls show, is far more circumspect than print—literature is largely a white-collar medium. The mass-circulated movie, intended for a heavily blue-collar drive-in audience, is far less erotic than the art film shown for middle-class audiences.

And so it goes. American censorship is a residue of Victorian attitudes, and is still directed primarily against the working-class male. Male sexual behavior remains a function of class, as the Kinsey reports amply documented. Even today white-collar boys think of blue-collar girls as fair game. If you get them in trouble you don't marry them; you simply give them some money.

Democracy has failed in America in many ways. One of them, certainly, is sexual. Sexual jealousy, sexual envy, sexual desire are as potent a combination of feelings as exists in man. As long as some in this society can say, "I can use your women, but you can't use mine," there is likely to be rioting and the shrill cry for vengeance in the streets.

The Language of
Prurient Interest

From *How to Talk Dirty and Influence People*
by Lenny Bruce

The first time I got arrested for obscenity was in San Francisco. I used a ten-letter word onstage. Just a word in passing.

"Lenny, I wanna talk to you," the police officer said. "You're under arrest. That word you said—you can't say that in a public place. It's against the law to say it and do it."

They said it was a favorite homosexual practice. Now that I found strange. I don't relate that word to a homosexual practice. It relates to any contemporary chick I know, or would know, or would love, or would marry.

Then we get into the patrol wagon, and another police officer says, "You know, I got a wife and kid . . ."

"I don't wanna hear that crap," I interrupted.

"Whattaya mean?"

"I just don't wanna hear that crap, that's all. Did your wife ever do that to you?"

"No."

"Did anyone?"

"No."

"Did you ever say the word?"

"No."

"You never said the word one time? Let ye cast the first stone, man."

"Never."

"How long have you been married?"

"Eighteen years."

"You ever chippied on your wife?"

"Never."

"Never chippied on your wife one time in eighteen years?"

"Never."

"Then I love *you* . . . because you're a spiritual guy, the kind of husband I would like to have been . . . but if you're lying, you'll spend some good time in purgatory . . ."

Now we get into court. They swear me in.

THE COP: "Your Honor, he said blah-blah-blah."

THE JUDGE: "He said *blah*-blah-blah! Well, I got grandchildren . . ."

Oh, Christ, there we go again.

"Your Honor," the cop says, "I couldn't believe it, there's a guy up on the stage in front of women in a mixed audience, saying blah-blah-blah . . ."

THE DISTRICT ATTORNEY: "Look at him, he's smug! I'm not surprised he said blah-blah-blah . . ."

"He'll probably say blah-blah-blah again, he hasn't learned his lesson . . ."

And then I dug something: they sort of *liked* saying blah-blah-blah.

(Even the BAILIFF:) "What'd he say?"

"He said blah-blah-blah."

"Shut up, you blah-blah-blah."

They were yelling it in the courtroom.

"Goddamn, it's good to say blah-blah-blah!"

The Language of Racism:
The English Language Is My Enemy

Ossie Davis

I stand before you, a little nervous, afflicted to some degree with stage fright. Not because I fear you, but because I fear the subject.

The title of my address is, "Racism in American Life—Broad Perspectives of the Problem," or, "The English Language Is My Enemy."

In my speech I will define culture as the sum total of ways of living built up by a group of human beings and transmitted by one generation to another. I will define education as the act or process of imparting and communicating a culture, developing the powers of reasoning and judgment and generally preparing oneself and others intellectually for a mature life.

I will define communication as the primary means by which the process of education is carried out.

I will say that language is the primary medium of communication in the educational process and, in this case, the English language. I will indict the English language as one of the prime carriers of racism from one person to another in our society and discuss how the teacher and the student, especially the Negro student, are affected by this fact.

The English language is my enemy.

Racism is a belief that human races have distinctive characteristics, usually involving the idea that one's own race is superior and has a right to rule others. Racism.

The English language is my enemy.

But that was not my original topic—I said that English was my goddamn enemy. Now why do I use "goddamn" to illustrate this aspect of the English language? Because I want to illustrate the sheer gut power of words. Words which control our actions. Words like "nigger," "kike," "sheeny," "dago," "black power"—words like this. Words we don't use in ordinary decent conversation, one to the other. I choose these words deliberately, not to flaunt my freedom before you. If you are a normal human being these words will have assaulted your senses, may even have done you physical harm, and if you so choose, you could have me arrested.

Those words are attacks upon your physical and emotional well-being; your pulse rate is possibly higher, your breath quicker; there is perhaps a tremor along the nerves of your arms and your legs; sweat begins in the palms of your hands, perhaps. With these few words I have assaulted you. I have damaged you, and there is nothing you can possibly, possibly do to control your reactions—to defend yourself against the brute force of these words.

These words have a power over us; a power that we cannot resist. For a moment you and I have had our deepest physical reactions controlled, not by our own wills, but by words in the English language.

A superficial examination of Roget's *Thesaurus of the English Language* reveals the following facts: The word "whiteness" has 134 synonyms, forty-four of which are favorable and pleasing to contemplate. For example: "purity," "cleanness," "immaculateness," "bright," "shiny," "ivory," "fair," "blonde," "stainless," "clean," "clear," "chaste," "unblemished," "unsullied," "innocent," "honorable," "upright," "just," "straightforward," "fair," "genuine," "trustworthy" —and only ten synonyms which I feel to have been negative and then only in the mildest sense, such as "gloss-over," "whitewash," "gray," "wan," "pale," "ashen," etc.

The word "blackness" has 120 synonyms, sixty of which are distinctly unfavorable, and none of them even mildly positive. Among the offending sixty were such words as "blot," "blotch," "smut," "smudge," "sullied," "begrime," "soot," "becloud," "obscure," "dingy," "murky," "low-toned," "threatening," "frowning," "foreboding," "forbidding," "sinister," "baneful," "dismal," "thundery," "wicked," "malignant," "deadly," "unclean," "dirty," "unwashed," "foul," etc. In addition, and this is what really hurts, twenty of those words—I exclude the villainous sixty above—are related directly to race, such as "Negro," "Negress," "nigger," "darkey," "blacka-moor," etc.

If you consider the fact that thinking itself is subvocal speech (in other words, one must use words in order to think at all), you will appreciate the enormous trap of racial pre-judgment that works on any child who is born into the English language.

Any creature, good or bad, white or black, Jew or Gentile, who uses the English language for the purposes of communi-cation is willing to force the Negro child into sixty ways to despise himself, and the white child, sixty ways to aid and abet him in the crime.

Language is a means of communication. This corruption, this evil of racism, doesn't affect only one group. It doesn't take white to make a person a racist. Blacks also become inverted racists in the process.

A part of our function, therefore, as teachers, will be to reconstruct the English language. A sizable undertaking, but one which we must undertake if we are to cure the problems of racism in our society.

The English language must become democratic. It must become respectful of the possibilities of the human spirit. Racism is not only reflected in words relating to the color of Negroes. If you will examine some of the synonyms for the word "Jew" you will find that the adjectives and the verb of the word "Jew" are offensive. However, if you look at the word "Hebrew" you will see that there are no offensive con-notations to the word.

When you understand and contemplate the small difference between the meaning of one word supposedly representing one fact, you will understand the power, good or evil, associated with the English language. You will understand also why there is a tremendous fight among the Negro people to stop using the word "Negro" altogether and substitute "Afro-American."

You will understand, even further, how men like Stokely Carmichael and Floyd McKissick can get us in such serious trouble by using two words together: Black Power. If Mr.

McKissick and Mr. Carmichael had thought a moment and said Colored Power, there would have been no problem.

We come today to talk about education. Education is the only valid transmitter of American values from one generation to another. Churches have been used from time immemorial to teach certain values to certain people, but in America, as in no other country, it is the school that bears the burden of teaching young Americans to be Americans.

Schools define the meaning of such concepts as success. And education is a way out of the heritage of poverty for Negro people. It's the way we can get jobs.

Education is that which opens that golden door that was so precious to Emma Lazarus. But education in the past has basically been built on the theory that we could find those gifted individuals among the Negro people and educate them out of their poverty, out of their restricted conditions, and then they would, in turn, serve to represent the best interests of the race; and if we concentrated on educating Negroes as individuals, we would solve the problem of discrimination by educating individual Negroes out of the problem. But I submit that that is a false and erroneous function and definition of education. We can no longer, as teachers, concentrate on finding the gifted black child in the slums or in the middle-class areas and giving him the best that we have. This no longer serves the true function of education if education indeed is to fulfill its mission to assist and perpetuate the drive of the Negro community to come into the larger American society on the same terms as all other communities have come.

Let us look for a brief moment at an article appearing in *Commentary* in February 1964, written by the associate director of the American Jewish Committee. "What is now perceived as the revolt of the Negro amounts to this," he says. "The solitary Negro seeking admission into the white world through unusual achievement has been replaced by the organized Negro insisting upon a legitimate share for his group of the goods of American society. The white liberal, in turn, who, whether or not he is fully conscious of it, has generally conceived of progress in race relations as the one-by-one assimilation of deserving Negroes into the larger society, now finds himself confused and threatened by suddenly having to come to terms with an aggressive Negro community that wishes to enter en masse.

"Accordingly, in the arena of civil rights, the Negro revolution has tended to take the struggle out of the courts and bring it to the streets and the negotiating tables. Granting the potential for unprecedented violence that exists here, it must also be borne in mind that what the Negro people are now beginning to do, other ethnic minorities who brought to America their strong traditions of communal solidarity did before them. With this powerful asset, the Irish rapidly acquired political strength and the Jews succeeded in raising virtually an entire immigrant population into the middle class within a span of two generations. Viewed in this perspective, the Negroes are merely the last of America's significant ethnic minorities to achieve communal solidarity and to grasp the role of the informal group power structure in protecting the rights and advancing the opportunities of the individual members of the community."

Liberal opinion in the North and in the South thus continues to stand upon its traditions of gradualism—that of one-by-one admission of deserving Negroes into the larger society and rejection of the idea that to help the Negro it must help first the Negro community.

Today in America, as elsewhere, the Negro has made us forcefully aware of the fact that the rights and privileges of an individual rest upon the status obtained by the group to which he belongs.

In the American pattern, where social power is distributed by groups, the Negro has come to recognize that he can achieve equal opportunities only through concerted action of the Negro community. We can't do it one by one any more; we must do it as a group.

Now, how is education related to the process not of lifting individuals but of lifting a whole group by its bootstraps and helping it climb to its rightful place in American society?

One of the ways is by calling such meetings as this to discuss Negro history—to discuss those aspects of Negro culture which are important for the survival of the Negro people as a community. There is nothing in the survival of the Negro people as a community that is inherently hostile to the survival of the interests of any other group.

So when we say Black Power and Black Nationalism we do not mean that that is the only power or that that is the only nationalism that we are concerned about or that it is to predominate above all others. We merely mean that it should have the right of all other groups and be respected as such in the American way of life.

Teachers have a very important function. They have before them the raw materials of the future. And if we were satisfied by the job that was being done in our country and in our culture it would not be necessary to call a protest conference. It would be necessary only to call a conference to celebrate.

I submit that racism is inherent in the English language because the language is an historic expression of the experience of a people; that racism, which is the belief that one group is superior to the other and has the right to set the standards for the other, is still one of the main spiritual policies of our country as expressed in the educational process.

Those of us who are concerned, those of us who are caught up, those of us who really want to be involved, must be prepared at this conference to tear aside our most private thoughts and prejudices, remembering that we have been taught them because we are all born to the English language.

Let us not feel personally guilty or personally responsible for the fact that we may not like Negroes. Let us remember that we are participating in the culture which has taught us not to like them, so that, when we are tempted to teach a child from above his position, or to say that "I represent white Anglo-Saxon gentility and culture, and out of the gratitude and graciousness of my heart I am going to reach down and lift you up to my level;" we know that is the incorrect attitude.

We cannot reach down and lift up any more, we must all get down together and reciprocate one to the other and come up together.

Let us, above all, be honest one to the other. Let us pursue truth though it hurts, though it makes us bleed. I said in the beginning that my purpose in using those lacerating words was to expose our innermost feeling. We must dig even deeper for the roots in our own consciousness, black and white, of the real fact of racism in our culture, and having faced that in ourselves, go back to the various schools from which we came and look upon the children before us as an opportunity, not only to practice the craft of teaching and the imparting of knowledge but, equally important, as an opportunity to learn from a subjugated people what its value, its history, its culture, its wealth as an independent people are. Let there be in our classrooms a sharing of the wealth of American democracy.

I have had occasion (and with this I'll come to a close) to function as a teacher—I'm a bootleg teacher, I teach Sunday school, it's the closest I can get to the process—I teach boys from nine to twelve, and I have the same problem with getting them to appreciate the spoken and written word, as you do, in your daily classrooms. Most of them can't read. I don't see how they're going to get, not only to heaven—I don't see how they're going to get to the next grade unless they can command some of these problems that we have.

But, more importantly, I am also involved in the educational process. And those of us who are involved in culture and cultural activities do ourselves and our country and our cause a great injustice not to recognize that we, too, are communicators and have therefore a responsibility in the process of communication. I could be hired today to communicate to the great American public my great delight in smoking a cigarette, but I know that a cigarette would cause you cancer and I could be paid for that. I could be used to do many other things in the process of communications from the top to the bottom.

I have a responsibility to show that what I do, what is translated through me, is measured by the best interest of my country and my people and my profession. And in that I think we are all together.

On Master-Baiting

Negro, *n,; pl.* NEGROES. [fr. L. *niger;* perh. akin to Greek *anigros* unclean, base] 1. A person belonging to the black race, esp. to the typical African branch of that race (formerly called the Ethiopian), the type being characterized by tall stature and often powerful physique, extreme dolichocephaly, convex forehead, prognathous jaws with large teeth, flat broad nose, everted lips, woolly hair, and dark-brown to sooty-black complexion.

—Webster's New International Dictionary (Second Edition)

And the power to define is the most important power we have. He is master who can define. That was made clear in the McCarthy period. If McCarthy said you were a Communist, you had to get up and say, No I am not a Communist. He had the power to define. It is the same thing. My fellow Americans, the Communists, the slanted-eye Vietcong are our enemy. You must go kill them. You don't have the right to define whether or not that cat is your enemy. The master has defined it for you. And when he says jump, you say, how high, boss?

—Stokely Carmichael at Morgan State College, Jan. 16, 1967

"But 'glory' doesn't mean 'a nice knockdown argument,' " Alice objected.

"When I use a word," Humpty Dumpty said in rather a scornful tone, "it means just what I choose it to mean— neither more nor less."

"The question is," said Alice, "whether you can make words mean so many different things."

"The question is," said Humpty Dumpty, "which is to be Master—that's all."

—Lewis Carroll, *Through the Looking-Glass*

Incident

Countee Cullen

Once riding in old Baltimore
   Heart-filled, head-filled with glee,
I saw a Baltimorean
   Keep looking straight at me.

Now I was eight and very small,
   And he was no whit bigger,
And so I smiled, but he poked out
   His tongue, and called me, "Nigger."

I saw the whole of Baltimore
   From May until December;
Of all the things that happened there
   That's all that I remember.

The Language of Self-Deception

Ashley Montagu

The way we talk about ourselves and our institutions, the way in which we use long-established "respectable" terms, leads us to make unrealistic and destructive evaluations of ourselves, of others, of the man-made world, and of the world of nature. It is seldom understood that the world we perceive is the world we see through words, that the world of experience is the world of arbitrarily conferred meanings. Each of us has learned to see the world not as it is but through the distorting glass of our words. It is through words that we are made human, and it is through words that we are dehumanized.

The meaning of a word is the action it produces. That is the operational definition of a word. Every member of a culture becomes a functioning member of that culture as a consequence of the behavior of others acting upon him. During the socialization process, that is, the process of being turned into a human being, the words are directed toward him with specific ends in view, and as the child becomes increasingly aware of the world around him, words, even though they are not specifically directed at him, continue to be the principal instruments which turn him upon the lathe of language into a growing human being. His behavior is shaped by words.

Words consist not merely of chopped-up segments of sounds having conventionalized meanings, but also of their accompaniments, such as kinesic movements of the body, principally of the face. Part or even the whole of the meaning of a word may be derived from the expression, the inflection, associated with it. Furthermore, words also derive a considerable part of this meaning from the environmental contexts in which they occur. For example, take the term *race*. When uttered with the malice, bigotry, and hatred of a Southern racist, the term differs very greatly from the meaning with which it is endowed when uttered by a scientist, however insubstantially, as a classificatory device. The term has a very different meaning in the home of a Georgia cracker from that which it has in a university classroom in which it is undergoing prolonged and critical examination. Words, in short, are the repositories of our experience. Their private and their public faces do not necessarily correspond, and they are accommodatable to changes in time and place. "Race" is a good example of such a word, for it is characterized by all sorts of private and public meanings, when in fact it corresponds to nothing whatever in reality. But no matter how confused or unreal the idea, a word can always be found to give a habitation and a name. The ambiguity of language is uniquely helpful in promoting confusion of thought, for with its assistance men are able to build their logic to fit their rationalizations, and most men's words are nothing but pseudo-logical rationalizations based on unanalyzed systems of values.

Men measure the value of words by the realities in which they believe, and since those realities are determined by the very words they believe in, the process is tautologically very satisfactory indeed. When the unreal is acted upon as if it were real it becomes, for all practical purposes, just as real as the real.

For most people, whether they are racists or not, the term "race" means that there exists something called "race" which determines the mental, behavioral, cultural abilities, and physical traits of different peoples. This colligation of differences is what the "true believer" understands by "race." The erroneous beliefs, attitudes, and conclusions and violent emotions that are enshrined in this term serve not only to maintain the doctrine of the inequality of man, but also to perpetuate the irrational practices which maintain the barriers between men. The fact that "race" corresponds to nothing in reality, that it represents a purely arbitrary classificatory device at best which many authorities consider wholly inapplicable to man, not to mention other creatures,[1] and at worst a wholly untenable confusion of ideas concerning the

[1] Ashley Montagu (ed.), *The Concept of Race,* New York, The Free Press, 1964; Ashley Montagu, *Man's Most Dangerous Myth: The Fallacy of Race* (4th ed.), Cleveland and New York, World Publishing Company, 1964.

nature of the physical traits, and the meaning of differences in individual and cultural achievement, is something that is wholly unknown to the hundreds of millions who believe in "race" as a real entity. Furthermore, when such "true believers" are exposed to the facts they are often utterly unimpressed by them. When exposed to the light their minds, like the pupils of their eyes, automatically contract. In addition, there are those who are able to accept the facts intellectually, but not emotionally. "I don't believe in ghosts," remarked Madame de Staël, "but I'm afraid of them." It is a common human response.

In what follows I shall consider a selection of words and phrases which are commonly used as if they had a biological or social validity or both; words and phrases which are more or less pervasive in their influence upon the thinking and the conduct mostly of the educated; words which for too long have conditioned and confused and misdirected the thinking and conduct of men in the Western world. There are literally hundreds of such words, phrases, and metaphors. I discuss here only a few of those with which I have myself been involved in attempting to clarify and criticize in the past.

Human Nature

Since people are so much in the midst of human nature most of us are authorities on the subject. The first of the errors almost universally committed is the assumption that human nature is something with which one is born. The fact is that one is no more born with human nature than one is born with speech. Both are potentialities which have to be learned. There are, of course, genetic limits, which are associated with those potentialities, but allowing for the full range of those limits, all members of the species *Homo sapiens* are capable of being humanized. And they are humanized according to the patterns of conditioning they undergo within their particular social group or culture. The enculturation of the individual is a continuous process of growth and development in the ability to interact with the world in which one develops, according to and with the learned forms of behavior prevailing in the culture. *That* is human nature. Hence, the vulgar practice of attributing a variety of usually unpleasant forms of human behavior to "human nature," as if that "human nature" constituted an hereditary or inborn endowment from which one cannot escape, is quite unsound.

What man is born with is a highly generalized capacity for learning, for educability. Educability is, indeed, the species characteristic of man. But what he will learn will depend, allowing for his genetic limitations, entirely upon the man-made part of the environment into which he is born and the manner in which it acts upon him to tailor him according to the pattern prevailing in that culture. Man, in short, is custom made.

It is not his nature, therefore, that requires attention, but his nurture. Let us cease blaming his faults upon the former, when they are in fact due to the latter.

Instinct

When one asks most people to define what they mean by "instinct" it is my experience that they are seldom able to do so and make any sense at all. The nearest most people get to a definition is to say that an instinct is an automatic response to a stimulus. This is incorrect. That is the definition of a reflex—a very different thing. Yet most people are sure that man is driven by many instincts. But the truth is that man has no instincts. An instinct is an inherited psychophysical disposition causing the organism to react upon the perception of a particular stimulus with a particular behavior or series of behaviors accompanied by a particular emotion. Man has no such endowments.

It makes things a lot easier to be able to attribute complex forms of behavior to innate mechanisms like "instincts," but while this may be satisfying to many people, it is very unsatisfying to those who are interested in discovering what the truth really is. And the truth, as is always the case, is vastly more interesting than the mythology which serves to obscure it.

Again, allowing for the genetic limits and differences which characterize every individual, all human behavior has to be learned. If we would understand any of man's behaviors our task must then be to study the conditions in which he acquired those behaviors. To attempt to trace those behaviors back to "instinctive" causes would be like searching for a nonexistent cat in a big dark room. It would divert attention from the real causes and focus them on an attention- and time-wasting procedure which would only lead to deeper confusion. This is precisely what such writers as Robert Ardrey, Konrad Lorenz, and Desmond Morris are succeeding in doing in their widely read books.[2] These books enjoy the wide appeal they do, not only because they serve to "explain" the aggressiveness of man, but because by attributing that aggressiveness to "human nature" and to "instinct," they relieve the reader of the burden of guilt he may have been carrying around for being as aggressive as he knows himself to be. For, he reasons, if he was born so, he can hardly be blamed for being so.

Aggressiveness

Aggressiveness is behavior designed to inflict pain upon another. The "authorities," such as Ardrey, Lorenz, and Morris, have informed us, as have innumerable "authorities" before them, that aggressive behavior is part of human nature, that it is instinctive. Hence, wars, juvenile delinquents, murderers, rapists, and violence will always be with us. Again, the truth is that aggressive behavior is always learned behavior provided by aggressive models who, under the appropriate conditions, are imitated. Aggression is almost invariably the response to frustration and, especially in the young, a reaction to the frustrated need for love.[3]

Misinterpretations of Darwin's discussions of "the struggle

[2] Robert Ardrey, *African Genesis,* New York: Atheneum, 1961; Robert Ardrey, *The Territorial Imperative,* New York, Atheneum, 1966; Konrad Lorenz, *On Aggression,* New York, Harcourt, Brace & World, 1966; Desmond Morris, *The Naked Ape,* New York, McGraw-Hill, 1968.

[3] Ashley Montagu, *The Direction of Human Development,* New York, Harper, 1955.

for existence," to which Darwin undeliberately contributed by the careless use of such phrases as "the warfare of nature," "the survival of the fittest," and the like, helped to create a pseudo-scientific basis for the belief that "Nature" was, as Tennyson had put it, "red in tooth and claw."[4] "Nature," actually the projection of nineteenth-century industrial Europe upon the screen of "the jungle" and "the wild," was conceived to be an arena in which the most successfully competitive reaped the rewards and the weakest went to the wall. This fitted very well the Protestant ethic of wealth as evidence of divine grace, and poverty the station to which its occupiers had been divinely appointed. It also fitted, like a glove, the world of laissez-faire competition, and the Social Darwinists' views of the relations of men, classes, and nations to each other.[5]

Hence, it was clear that aggression was virtually part of the nature of things. Aggression was a law of nature. This only goes to show how easily men mistake their prejudices for the laws of nature, and how seldom they realize that all the laws of nature are man-made laws, and only too often are completely artifactual.

The belief in "innate depravity," in the natural aggressiveness of man, has influenced religious teachings and practice, education, law, military theoreticians, and would-be reformers, not to mention businessmen in their relations with their competitors and their employers, as well as their customers.

It is perhaps significant that criminologists, one of the few professional people who have been disinclined to believe in "innate depravity," enjoy possibly the best of opportunities to know what a large part environmental factors have played in the history of the lives of those convicted of aggressive crimes.

If any progress is ever to be made in controlling and reducing the development of aggressive behavior in man, it will be

[4] Ashley Montagu, *Darwin, Competition, and Cooperation,* New York, Schuman, 1953.
[5] Richard Hofstadter, *Social Darwinism in American Thought 1860–1915,* Boston, Beacon Press, 1965.

necessary to recognize its causes for what they are. Those causes are mainly, if not entirely, environmental. To divert attention from this fact is to do a disservice to the cause of human progress.

The Law of the Jungle

This Victorian idea is closely associated with the rise of Darwinism and such other related ideas as "The Struggle for Existence," "The Survival of the Fittest," "The race is to the swift," "The strongest survive; the weakest go to the wall," "Might is Right," and many others of a similar sort. "Nature" was conceived to be in a continuous state of conflict, and "the jungle," a gladiatorial struggle in which no quarter was given.

We see, it has been said, according to the kingdom that is within us, and as I have already remarked, this view of "Nature," of "the jungle," represented nothing more nor less than the projection of man's own crippled image of himself and the frightfulness of his own societies upon the screen of "Nature." Such a view of Nature not only justified the ways of man to his fellow men, not only served to explain them, even though deprecatorily, but also served to justify the ways of man in his ruthless destruction of "Nature" for his own ends. Thus, the application of "The Law of the Jungle" against its inhabitants was considered a just punishment for their brutishness and cruelty, and the cropping out of such behavior toward his fellow man was considered one of those unavoidable expressions of "human nature" due to man's own ancestry of brutishness and cruelty. "The Law of the Jungle" seemed to be a "Law of Nature" which, do what he would, man found difficulty in escaping.

These misbegotten ideas are closely related to that other confusion of pathogenic ideas enshrined in what I have called "The Myth of the Beast." This is the idea that "lower" animals are cruel and ferocious by "nature." Hence, their extermination is an act of grace which serves to reduce the quantity of cruelty and danger that exists in the world. Hence, anyone who chooses to do so may arm himself with some lethal weapon and take the life of any number of "wild" animals he chooses.

The truth is that there are no jungles or wild animals except in the cities which men have created; that the view of "nature," of "the wild," and of "wild animals" that men have created represents a libel and a caricature of the realities. These views serve to distort and impoverish the world of humanity and of nature, and what is worse, to justify the destruction of both humanity and nature.

The "Lower" Animals

Other animals by virtue of the fact that they are different are classified as "lower." But they are not "lower," they are merely different. Certainly men can do some things better than other animals, but then virtually every other animal can do a great many things a great deal better than any man can do. Every animal is adapted to its particular niche, and most animals have occupied their particular niches considerably longer than man has his. Man's anthropocentrism, however, is such that, having awarded himself all the prizes and elected himself to the topmost rung of the "scale of nature," he can afford to look down with pride in himself and contempt for all other animals, for is he not *Homo sapiens,* the "wise guy," the first amidst the Order of Mammals, *Primates*? It was Oscar Wilde who described man's naming himself *Homo sapiens* as perhaps the most oafishly arrogant definition of a species ever given. However that may be, man combining his myth making with his taxonomic faculty has become the creator and caretaker of his own classificatory system in which he has elected himself to the top and placed other animals on a descending series of rungs upon the "scale of nature."

The conception of "lower animals" is closely related to the idea of "lower races." Because other ethnic groups differ in various ways from ourselves they are therefore regarded as "inferior" and we, the classifiers, as "superior." When we inquire into the causes of the differences we find that the classifier's prejudices enable him to find a ready explanation for them in "heredity" or "innate factors," when, in fact, the differences have a vastly more interesting explanation than that, and have nothing whatever to do with questions of superiority or inferiority. Both physical and behavioral traits are due to differences in the physical and cultural history of the different groups.

Differences in the challenges of the physical environment have elicited genetic reactions which have adaptively served to fit the organism to live in an environment of such challenges, whether of sunlight intensity, humidity, the presence of malaria-bearing mosquitoes, and the like. Dark-pigmented skin is at an advantage in high-sunlight areas. In such areas it is definitely adaptively superior to white skin. But a highly developed intelligence enables light-skinned people to stay out of the sun. Such intelligence is also an evolutionary product of adaptive value.

Similarly, differences in behavior and in cultural achievement are due not to differences in genes but to differences in the history of experience which each group and each individual has undergone, to differences in the storage of acquired traits, namely, culture.

It is not to genetic heredity but to social heredity that man owes his equipment of behavioral traits. That equipment will differ according to the characteristics of the culture in which it has been acquired. There is no such thing as the inheritance of acquired physical characteristics. But behaviorally there is very definitely such a thing as the inheritance of acquired social traits—not from a genetic heredity but from a social heredity.

Heredity

Most people take "heredity" to mean something equivalent to predestination—a view which has done a considerable amount of harm. More explicitly, what "heredity" has been taken to mean by many who should have known better is that it is something that is determined at fertilization; something we derive from our parents in our genes which determines our physical traits and largely our behavioral characteristics.

This is a wholly confused and unsound view of heredity.

Heredity is neither something that is determined at conception nor something that we are born with. In fact, heredity determines nothing. What the genes do, *under the stimulation of the environments in which they interact and develop,* is influence the physiological and behavioral development of traits. Genes do not act, they interact with one another and in the environments which act upon them. There is no interaction of genes with anything unless there are environmental actions upon them. Thus, what the organism develops as is dependent upon two principal interactive factors: 1) the genes, and 2) the environments. Heredity is the expression of the interaction between genes and environments in which they have undergone development. Hence, the end result of that expression, the phenotype, is not something that has been determined by genes or by anything else, but has been *influenced* to develop as it has as a consequence of the differences in the interactions which have occurred between unique aggregates of genes and particular kinds of environments.

Heredity is a dynamic interactive series of processes, *not* a static condition. Heredity is *not* predestination. It is not something about which one can do nothing. On the contrary, it is something about which one can do a great deal. By varying either the genes or the environments or both, one can greatly influence the expression of traits. This is readily seen in matters of health, growth, development, intelligence, learning ability, behavior, achievement, and the like.[6]

Discussions as to whether heredity or environment is "stronger" are, in the light of the facts, completely nonsensical. What is important always to remember is that there are no genes without an environment, and what the genes can do the environment can also do, but alone neither can do anything.

[6] Ashley Montagu, *Human Heredity,* Cleveland and New York, World Publishing Company, 1965; Gladys C. Schwesinger, *Heredity and Environment,* New York, Macmillan, 1933; Jenny Hirsch (ed.), *Behavior—Genetic Analysis,* New York, McGraw-Hill, 1967; Max Levitan and Ashley Montagu, *Fundamentals of Human Genetics,* New York, Oxford University Press, 1968.

Blood and Consanguinity

Blood as the quintessential element of the body which carries, and through which are transmitted, the hereditary qualities of the stock is a persisting archaism which has, for example, forced the Red Cross to segregate Negro blood banks from white blood banks, and societies to distinguish between "royal blood," "blue blood," "foreign blood," and the blood of commoners. Except for the great variability in its groups, types, and other serological characters, all human blood is of one and the same kind, and no blood carries hereditary "determinants." The hereditary factors are carried in the genes, which are situated in the chromosomes, and nowhere else. The blood of aristocrats, royalty, foreigners, and ordinary men and women is of the same kind and indistinguishable from one another. There is no such thing as blue blood. Nor is there any such thing as "consanguinity," for the simple reason that human beings cannot be related by "blood" but only by genes.

"Good blood," "bad blood," "fullblood," "halfblood," are all scientifically nonsensical terms. The official philosopher of the Nazis, Alfred Rosenberg, declared that "this recognition of the profound significance of blood is now mysteriously encircling our planet, irresistibly gripping one nation after the other." [7] And, indeed, with this belief the Nazis carried out a murderous blood bath such as the world had never even imagined possible. As Voltaire remarked, those who believe in absurdities will not find it difficult to commit atrocities.

Miscegenation

The term *miscegenation* provides a remarkable exhibit in the natural history of nonsense. The term is used in a pejorative sense as referring to "race mixture." The prefix *mis* (from the Latin *miscere,* mix) has probably contributed its share to the misunderstanding of the nature of "race" mixture. Words that begin with the prefix *mis* suggest "mistake," "misuse,"

---

[7] *Vossiche Zeitung,* September 3, 1933.

"mislead," and similar erroneous ideas implying wrong conduct.

The word *miscegenation* was invented as a hoax, and published in an anonymous pamphlet in New York in 1864, with the title *Miscegenation: The Theory of the Blending of the Races, Applied to the White Man and Negro.*[8] The pamphlet was almost certainly the joint product of two members of the New York *World* staff, David Goodman Croly, an editor, and George Wakeman, one of the reporters. The purpose of the authors was to raise the "race" issue in aggravated form in the 1864 presidential campaign by attributing to the abolitionist Republican party the views set forth in *Miscegenation.* The pamphlet was intended to commit the Republican leaders to "the conclusions to which they are brought by their own principles," without any hope of success but in the expectation that their folly would be made all the more clear to them in granting the Negro the franchise. The brief introduction sets the tone of the whole pamphlet.

"The word is spoken at last. It is Miscegenation—the blending of the various races of men—the practical recognition of all the children of the common father. While the sublime inspirations of Christianity have taught this doctrine, Christians so-called have ignored it in denying social equality to the colored man; while democracy is founded upon the idea that all men are equal, democrats have shrunk from the logic of their own creed, and refuse to fraternize with the people of all nations. . . ." And much else, with tongue in cheek, to the same effect.

The word *miscegenation* is defined by the authors as follows: "*Miscegenation*—from the Latin *Miscere,* to mix, and *Genus,* race, is used to denote the abstract idea of the mixture of two or more races."

Thus, the word *miscegenation* was invented by satirists to replace the vulgar term *amalgamation,* as not being sufficiently elevated or distinguished.

---

[8]This pamphlet is the subject of an excellent little book by J. M. Bloch, *Miscegenation, Meloleukation, and Mr. Lincoln's Dog,* Schaum, 1958.

Indeed, the word does carry with it a sort of authoritative aura, implying, however, a certain lack of respectability and even responsibility. The extent of the prejudice inherent in and engendered by this word may be gathered from the fact that Webster's New International Dictionary (Second Edition) defines "miscegenator" as "one who is *guilty* of miscegenation." The italics are mine. Former President Harry S Truman, when asked whether he thought "racial" intermarriages would become widespread in the United States, replied, "I hope not. I don't believe in it. What's that word about four feet long? Miscegenation?"[9]

Atavism

As a sorry example of the folly of falling into folk error, Webster scores again with *atavism.* Webster attributes the occurrence of an atavism to "recombination of ancestral genes." This lends the definition an aura of scientific respectability which it in fact wholly lacks. Such a "recombination of ancestral genes" simply never occurs and atavisms are simply creations of the imagination. Derived from the Latin *atavus,* an ancestor, the word appears to have been first used in English by James Rennie in 1833, writing, "Children often resemble their grandfathers or grandmothers more than their immediate parents. . . . This propensity is termed Atavism by Duchesne."[10] In this sense the word would have had a perfectly legitimate meaning and usage. But it suffered a change during the rise of evolutionary biology in the later half of the nineteenth century when it came to have the meaning of a reversion or throwback to an ancestral evolutionary condition. From biology the term was taken over for further service by literary men and writers in general. This is unfortunate because the word refers to a purely mythical series of events as if they were matters of fact.

When structures or functions occur which resemble those

---

[9] *The New York Times,* September 12, 1963.
[10] James Rennie, *The Science of Gardening,* Condon, 1833, p. 113.

which existed among ancestral groups, but have been lost by descendant groups, the trait, like a fistula in the neck which is homologized with the gill slits of a fish, or a tail-like structure, is not due to a "recombination of ancestral genes" but to abnormal developmental changes resulting in either persistence, suppression, reduction, hypertrophy, duplication, or multiplication of structures. A fistula in the neck has nothing to do developmentally or in any other way with the gill slits of fishes, but everything to do with an arrest of development at an early embryonic stage of the branchial arches.

It is apparent, then, that the words we use act as psychophysical conditioners which determine the manner in which the individual shall think, feel, and behave. Hence, the importance of sound-thinking and right-feeling, familial and educational goals. Hence, also, the importance of teaching language not so much as grammar but as behavior, of teaching language as a fine and delicate instrument of expression designed to put man into touch with his fellow man.

The Language of Survival
(Circa 1968)

"The first step in preparing the shelter for occupancy is to selectively recruit, train, and assign shelter management personnel to key management positions. . . . Although pre-emergency selection and assignment of a management cadre is desirable, it may be necessary to recruit most of the management staff from the shelter population after the shelter is put to use."

—p. 3

"Disturbances, conflicts and disorders may be prevented or minimized by: Immediate and forceful corrective action, particularly in the case of serious violations such as assault, revolt against authority, and so on."

—pp. 21–22

"Bodies of persons who die in shelter should be moved away from the occupied portion of the shelter and be placed in unused rooms, upper floors, or outside the shelter for later removal or burial."

—p. 24

"Within groups, persons should be separated on the basis of sex, age, and marital status. Single men may be separated from single women by the simple expedient of placing the men at one end of the sleeping area and the women at the other, with family groups in between."

—p. 28

"Spiritual activities within the shelter should reflect the thinking and wishes of the shelter population."

—p. 29

Excerpts from *Handbook for Shelter Management,*
Department of Defense, Office of Civil Defense

The Language of Advertising

Ronald Gross

The language of ads is language used to sell, language on the make. Its charms and its dangers, like those of the good-hearted whore whose most ambitious goal is a fur coat, are real but not of ultimate consequence. No man was ever importantly ruined by his infatuation for a whore: it's the mistresses we really love who rend our lives. So with language: the trivial choices between brands which the advertisers frantically seek to influence are of little significance beside the political and religious credos with which the ideologists ravish our minds and hearts.

Veblen, knowing this, dismissed advertising language as a mere "trading on the range of human infirmities." When F. R. Leavis surveyed the subject in 1934 in *Culture and Environment,* he concurred with Veblen. The ads he examined appealed mainly to petty greed, mean fears of social inferiority, anxieties about health, etc.

In the past twenty years the advertisers' repertoire of incantations has been augmented by some fumbling applications of behaviorism and Freudianism, the chief stratagems being repetition and sexual suggestiveness. But the ultimate aim is still merely to wheedle out of us a few greasy quarters or dollars. The ultimate consequences of switching from one toothpaste to another, or even from one automobile to another, are hardly momentous in themselves.

Why, then, is it worth while to scrutinize the language of advertising? Because the pathologies of language evident in advertising are now carrying over into other, more important, areas of our lives. As Galbraith points out, the breeding of delusory "images" has spread from the area of marketing to that of domestic and foreign policy, and thus colors our entire national life with a hue of unreality.

In a time like ours, when the mind is under constant semantic siege, every man must undertake what Daniel Boorstin calls "the task of disenchantment." Advertising language is not a bad place to start, though when we have penetrated its stratagems and discerned its obfuscations, we shall only be started on the road to mastery of the language environment.

Ads add. On that fact rests the entire semantic interest of advertising. If ads just gave us information about products, they would be of no use whatever to the semanticist, the cultural critic, or the social scientist. But precisely because ads bear only the flimsiest relationship to their ostensible subjects—the products—they are interesting.

Why do ads add? For the simplest possible reason—want of anything else to say about the product. There being no significant difference between two competing cigarettes or rolls of toilet paper, advertisers must fabricate a subject matter for their advertisement other than the product itself. What shall it be?

The answer is dictated by the major constraint under which the copywriter works: that his words must influence the largest possible number of people. The subject matter, then, will be what most people have in common—their basic fears, anxieties, and hopes. In short, our style of life, our values.

What ads add is *us*. Around the anonymous commodity— the bare roll of toilet paper, the unbranded cigarette, the purely chemical motor oil—the adman weaves his congeries of emotions. His raw materials are not the product's characteristics, but our own drives and aspirations. People must be made to want this object, not for what it is, but for what language can endow it with, for what it can be made to *mean*. The ad, in short, is a Rorschach blot onto which advertisers contrive to make us project some of our most pervasive and controlling attitudes. Advertising generally constitutes a vast collective Rorschach, an inchoate medium onto which advertiser and consumer project one another's fantasies and fears.

What better materials could there be for studying the patterns of appeal, persuasion, and ingratiation which operate in one's culture, the hopes, fears, and anxieties which haunt its inhabitants, than to look into these works of impure artifice? Before we put down the plethora of advertising which affronts us on every side, then, we should seize out of it those insights about the temper and the fever of the society in which we live. To close our eyes to these figments is to remain even more in the dark about the fears and hopes which drive our fellow countrymen in their groping toward some kind of human satisfaction.

Shelley's pronouncement that "Poets are the unacknowledged legislators of the world" seems preposterous to us because we think of poetry as being what's in books of poems. But semanticist S. I. Hayakawa has pointed out that advertising copywriters are the sponsored poets of our time, the laureates of a consumer society. Thus Shelley's dictum becomes merely a noble restatement of the documentary accounts of advertising one finds in Vance Packard, et al. The advertisers, not in their overt messages and their "power" to shape consumer preferences but in the underlying vision of man and of human life which they purvey, certainly shape attitudes and aspirations in just such a way. Shortly after the 1967 summer riots in the Negro ghettos, Bayard Rustin wrote in *The New York Times Magazine:* "If those Negro youths who rioted thought that a man was nothing if he didn't have an alpaca sweater and suede shoes—who taught them that?"

But here again, we must make an important distinction. Poets—and of course Shelley would include among them Plato and Kant and Marx—give us new images of man and of life, which widen our sensibilities. Advertisers help reinforce such images, but they do not create them in their important aspects. Rather, they slavishly search out pre-existing models to follow. Far from being bold mind-shapers, advertisers are timid to an appalling degree.

For example, motivational research revealed a few years ago that most people brush their teeth only once a day, "at the most pointless moment possible in the entire twenty-four-hour day from the dental-hygiene standpoint." Here was a small but real opportunity for advertisers. Armed with this intelligence they could have combined public usefulness with profit-making by trying to educate the public to their brand as well as to better habits which would detract from no one's profits. Rather than undertaking such a modest exercise in changing behavior, however, the agencies—snapping up the fact that people only brushed their teeth to get the crummy early-morning taste out of their mouths—elevated "tingly-taste" flavor and "clean mouth" breath-sweetening to No. 1 on their list of copy points.

The distinction between the overt effects of advertising language and the far more important side effects can be seen most clearly if we look at the interesting case of "good ads." Here the overt message is widely agreed to be beneficial, yet the underlying assumptions are pernicious. And their perniciousness derives from the same source as it does in all American advertising: the basic system of ideas which governs our society and economy. *The most basic dire effect of advertising, in short, lies in its affirmation of "the American way of life."*

Consider the prime example of "good ads": those dull, worthy campaigns of the Advertising Council. Financed by the industry, and operating through free space donated by the media, the council self-righteously advances behind its musty colophon of a quill pen crossed over a drawn saber, pressing on us that most repellent of commodities, good advice. When and as unfilled advertising space permits, the council reminds us to attend church, use the litter baskets, and retrain ourselves as automation gobbles up our jobs. Surely nothing could be more innocent.

But the whole business is something more than a bore: it is also a subtle medium for obfuscating some important public issues and reducing the likelihood of needed action. Not consciously, I imagine—that would credit the people behind the enterprise with more savvy than they probably have. But unconsciously, subliminally, and by default.

Take a recent ad. It shows an electric circuit, suitably baffling to the layman. "What are you going to do," asks the copy, "when this circuit learns your job?" The implication is clear: get off your ass, you sluggard. Retrain thyself—prepare.

We're doing you the service of giving you fair warning—but you'd better get a move on.

Buy why, one might ask, is the responsibility fixed so unerringly on the individual worker? Don't the businessman, the union, and government have any identifiable responsibility to prospective displaced workers when that circuit is installed? One can't imagine signs directed at businessmen which said: "What will happen to your workers when this circuit takes their jobs?" Again, intervention by the government to provide jobs for those displaced by automation is neglected as a possible remedy. Suddenly, in this campaign, the individual worker seems to have taken on all the responsibility for the epochal industrial transformation which our society is fumbling through.

Of course, a single car card can't do everything. "This is just one approach to the problem." But if you recall the council campaigns from the past few years, a somewhat sinister pattern emerges quite clearly. First, there's a problem: the streets are filthy; there's a ghastly death toll on the highways; colleges need more money.

Now, each of these problems is complex and has many possible and probably partial solutions. For instance, filthy streets might be remedied by greater expenditures for public sanitation services; deaths on the highway suggest that cars might be structurally unsafe; higher education's needs perhaps require federal aid to universities.

In the council's campaigns, however, such solutions are consistently neglected in favor of pinning the responsibility for action on the individual citizen: don't litter the streets; drive safely; give to the college of your choice. Clearly, each of these will contribute to the end desired. Equally clearly, however, other changes are mandatory—changes which challenge powerful vested interests in the society. Ralph Nader made it clear, for example, that the development and adaptation of a safer car by the automobile industry is a quicker and surer way to reduce traffic deaths than is the gigantic campaign to teach people to drive more carefully.

Such solutions don't commend themselves to the Advertising Council. Rather, it hammers away at the unprovocative, anonymous individual—if he'd just shape up, things would be fine. This country could solve its problems handily, the council ads seem to suggest, if it weren't for that sloppy, lazy, stingy, frivolous, uncivic, obdurate element—its people.

While no man was ever importantly ruined by a whore, the practice of debauchery on a continuous, society-wide basis certainly would have a demoralizing effect. And this is the important thing to say about the language of advertising. Although the choices which the advertisers seek to shape with their words are trivial, the side effects which permeate our society are ominous. They amount to nothing less than unremitting reinforcement, through ubiquitousness and repetition, of a demeaning conception of man, life, and the world.

The Language of Education
The Great Trivia Contest

Terence P. Moran

Who was the first actor to win an Academy Award in a starring role? A silver bullet is used as an identifying symbol by (a) Tom Mix, (b) the Durango Kid, (c) the Lone Ranger, (d) Hopalong Cassidy. For what studio did Humphrey Bogart make most of his major movies? Fibber McGee was famous for (a) his courage, (b) his musical talents, (c) his closet, (d) his friendship with Calvin Coolidge. Can you name two television series which featured Robert Rockwell?

Trivial questions? What do they have to do with the "language of education"? Then try these questions:

Who was the first American writer to win the Nobel prize for literature? A silver bullet ends the life of the principal character in (a) *Orpheus Descending,* (b) *The Emperor Jones,* (c) *The Silver Cord,* (d) *The Great God Brown.* Who published the first edition of Shakespeare's plays? Mrs. Malaprop was famous for (a) her beauty, (b) her patronage of the arts, (c) her misuse of the English language, (d) her friendship with Sir Philip Sidney. Can you name two plays written by John Webster?

The Random House Dictionary of the English Language defines "trivia" as "matters or things that are very unimportant, inconsequential, or inessential; trifles; trivialities." The word itself comes to us from the Latin *trivium,* a place where three roads meet and where conversation was limited to "small talk." In classical education students studied the trivium—grammar, rhetoric, and logic—thereby establishing the first connections between the trivium and trivia.

If the questions asked about the Academy Award, the silver bullet, Humphrey Bogart's studio, Fibber McGee's fame, and Robert Rockwell's television shows are trivial—of little importance or consequence—into what category shall we place the questions about the Nobel prize, the second silver bullet,

103

Shakespeare's publisher, Mrs. Malaprop's fame, and John Webster's plays? Why, into education, of course. While we recognize the triviality of the first set of questions, most of us fail to recognize the same triviality in the second. Such questions are what all too frequently pass for education in our society.

The sad truth seems to be that the language of education is largely the language of trivia. It is not without significance that the current game of Trivia sprang full-blown from the minds of our university students. Karl Marx once wrote that historical events occur twice, once in tragedy and once in farce. Given the state of American education today, it seems that the game of Trivia is the farcical counterpart to the tragedy of education.

For those who find this comparison of education to Trivia a bit strained, a bit far-fetched, I invite you to recall your own experiences in school. How do you rate yourself on these questions: (1) Who discovered America? (2) Who was the first man to circumnavigate the globe? (3) Who were the first men to explore the Mississippi River? (4) Who was the first President of the United States? (5) Who was the "Father of the American Navy"?

Are these legitimate history questions or trivia? I need not labor the point that what we call "America" had been inhabited long before Columbus, St. Brendan or Leif Ericson set foot on the place. Not only are such questions trivial in nature; they are racist in spirit, in that they contain a built-in assumption that nothing is "discovered" until it is stumbled upon by a European.

If you find the question "What were the names of the three horses ridden by Hopalong Cassidy, Eddie Dean, and Gene Autry?" to be trivia, what do you make of the question, "What were the names of the three ships that sailed to America with Columbus?"

Without doubt you were made to memorize the names of Columbus's ships in school; perhaps you remembered the names of the horses from Saturday movie shows. What is it in the questions that makes one part of a parlor game played for fun and the other part of a curriculum studied supposedly for education? It assuredly is not in the forms of the questions, since they are identical; it patently cannot be in the kinds of "learning" involved, since they are identical; it can only be that educators have decided, for some mysterious reasons, that it is worth while to know the names of the ships.

But why not learn the name of Hoppy's horse? Surely that is knowledge worth having. In my neighborhood a kid could achieve a hell of a lot more status among his peers (as the social scientists like to call guys you hang around with) if he reeled off "Topper, Copper, and Champion" than if he said "the *Nina,* the *Pinta,* and the *Santa Maria.*" If you answer that some facts are more important to know than others, I would agree; but I would ask you in return, "More important for what, and to whom?"

Make no mistake about it; knowledge of trivia brings fame, success, and reward in our culture. Whether it's a guy who wins beers in the corner bar because he can name the original Dead End Kids, a Charles Van Doren who achieves fame from answering questions on "Twenty-One," or a high-school student who can answer the teacher's questions about who wrote "The Highwayman" and "My Last Duchess," our entire system pays dividends for knowledge of trivia. What passes for a "good student" in our schools is usually that student who has memorized the most trivia thought important by the teacher.

I invite you to compare two sets of questions about various subjects. What differences do you find between the two sets? Which set seems more justified to be included in the curricula of our schools?

Science

1a. The scientist who first synthesized DNA was (a) Kornberg, (b) Sanger, (c) Ochoa, (d) du Vigneaud.

1b. The actor who first played Dr. Frankenstein in the movies was (a) Boris Karloff, (b) Bela Lugosi, (c) Colin Clive, (d) Basil Rathbone.

2a. Of the following, the scientist who originated and developed the system of classifying the plants and animals of the earth was (a) Linnaeus, (b) Darwin, (c) Mendel, (d) Agassiz.

2b. Of the following, the actor who originated the role of Tarzan in the movies was (a) Johnny Weissmuller, (b) Buster Crabbe, (c) Elmo Lincoln, (d) Herman Brix.

Social Science

1a. With which of the following is the "iron law of wages" most closely associated? (a) David Ricardo, (b) Leon Walrus, (c) Adam Smith, (d) Karl Marx.

1b. With which of the following is the saying "a friend to those who have no friends, an enemy to those who make him an enemy" most closely associated? (a) Charlie Chan, (b) Bulldog Drummond, (c) Boston Blackie, (d) Sherlock Holmes.

2a. If the names Joseph Schumpeton, Wesley Mitchell, and A. F. Burns were mentioned in a discussion, the subject under discussion would most likely be (a) money and banking, (b) business cycles, (c) housing, (d) Social Security.

2b. If the names Benson Fong, Mantan Moreland, and Willie Best were mentioned in a discussion, the subject under discussion would most likely be (a) race relations, (b) the United Nations, (c) crime detection (d) World War II.

3a. *Patterns of Culture* was written by (a) Margaret Mead, (b) Ruth Benedict, (c) Ralph Linton, (d) Ashley Montagu.

3b. "Terry and the Pirates" was created by (a) Hal Foster, (b) George Wunder, (c) Milton Caniff, (d) Ham Fisher.

At this point you may be thinking something like, "Yes, all this may be true for history, for geography, for science. After all, there are many facts that have to be learned in these areas. But the humanities are different; that's where students come to grips with ideas and concepts, where they learn to think creatively." My only answer is to invite you to continue with the test.

Philosophy

1a. Schiller, James, and Dewey are associated with (a) pragmatism, (b) deism, (c) positivism, (d) fascism.

1b. Solomon, Hercules, Atlas, Zeus, Achilles, and Mercury are associated with (a) *The Iliad,* (b) *The Odyssey,* (c) Captain Marvel, (d) The Ecumenical Movement.

2a. The last two hours of Socrates are described in (a) "The Two Fundamental Problems of Ethics," (b) "Phaedo," (c) "Rebellion of the Masses," (d) "Metaphysics of Morals."

2b. Freedonia's struggle for freedom is described in (a) *Horse Feathers,* (b) *Birth of a Nation,* (c) *Duck Soup,* (d) *Gone with the Wind.*

3a. "Catharsis" means a (a) purging, (b) lengthening, (c) reduction, (d) flippancy.

3b. "Ungawa" means (a) come, (b) go, (c) help, (d) all of the above, plus.

4a. One of the best known of the Cynics was (a) Diogenes, (b) Santayana, (c) Plato, (d) Rousseau.

4b. One of the best known of the Keystone Cops was (a) Milton Sills, (b) Harold Lloyd, (c) Ford Sterling, (d) Sessue Hayakawa.

5a. The Lyceum is associated with (a) Hegel, (b) Apuleius, (c) Marx, (d) Aristotle.

5b. Lompoc is associated with (a) Charlie Chaplin, (b) Stan Laurel, (c) W. C. Fields, (d) the Marx Brothers.

6a. "God is without passions, neither is he affected by any emotion of pleasure or pain"—expresses a phase of the religious philosophy of (a) Luther, (b) Spinoza, (c) Hume, (d) Emerson.

6b. "Never apologize; it's a sign of weakness"—expresses a phase in the life philosophy of (a) Richard Nixon, (b) Hideki Tojo, (c) John Wayne, (d) Ronald Reagan.

Are these the burning questions that students of philosophy should concern themselves with? Is this the examination Socrates had in mind when he said, "The unexamined life is not worth living"? To those who object on the grounds that some factual knowledge is a necessary prerequisite for more creative thinking, that details must be mastered before problem-solving begins, I maintain that few, if any, students (or teachers for that matter) ever go beyond the Trivia-Game stage of learning. Few education systems—whether on the primary or secondary, undergraduate or graduate level—spend considerable time on any aspect of education besides trivia questions.

If education is committed to trivia questions in the sciences, the social sciences, and philosophy, it is *dedicated* to such questions in the area of literature. Far from liberating the creative spirit of the students, most teachers of English sacrifice their students' creativity on the altar of the God of Trivia.

Literature

1a. "Thou shalt see me at Philippi" is the warning of (a) Hamlet's father to Hamlet, (b) Caesar's ghost to Brutus, (c) Antony to Cleopatra, (d) Tybalt to Romeo.

1b. "Even he who is pure in heart and says his prayers by night can become a wolf when the wolfbane blooms and the autumn moon is bright" is the warning given to (a) Clyde Beatty, (b) Lawrence Talbot, (c) Conrad Veidt, (d) Alf Landon.

2a. Dora Spendow, Steerforth, and Mr. Murdstone are characters in (a) *Seventeen,* (b) *David Copperfield,* (c) *Tom Jones,* (d) *Jane Eyre.*

2b. Titus Moody, Senator Claghorn, and Mrs. Nussbaum, are characters in (a) "Life with Luigi," (b) "Amos 'n' Andy," (c) "Allen's Alley," (d) "Out Our Way."

3a. A novel that presents a picture of clerical life in a cathedral town is (a) *Barchester Towers,* (b) *Middlemarch,* (c) *Wuthering Heights,* (d) *Vanity Fair.*

3b. A radio show that asked the question, "Can a young girl from a mining town in the West find happiness as the wife of England's richest and most handsome lord?" was (a) "Helen Trent," (b) "Mary Noble," (c) "Our Gal Sunday," (d) "Stella Dallas."

4a. The term "Malapropism" is associated with (a) Wilde, (b) Sheridan, (c) Congreve, (d) Shaw.

4b. The term "Kemo Sabe" is associated with (a) Tarzan, (b) Ramar, (c) Tonto, (d) Jungle Jim.

5a. The writer whose declared purpose was to "justify the ways of God to man" was (a) Jonathan Edwards, (b) Mathew Arnold, (c) John Bunyan, (d) John Milton.

5b. The crime fighter whose declared purpose was to "defend with equal vigor the rights and privileges of all . . . citizens" was (a) Boston Blackie, (b) The Green Hornet, (c) Mr. District Attorney, (d) the Public Defender.

6a. Of the following, the author who has not written a major work dealing with Thomas à Becket is (a) Jean Anouilh, (b) Alfred Duggan, (c) Evelyn Waugh, (d) T. S. Eliot.

6b. Of the following, the actor who has not played Frankenstein's monster in a movie is (a) Lon Chaney, Jr., (b) Bela Lugosi, (c) John Carradine, (d) Boris Karloff.

I could continue *ad infinitum,* and *ad nauseam,* but I trust the point is made well enough: the language of education and the language of Trivia are identical. The only difference seems to be in what educators decide to call "significant" at any given moment in history. I fail to see how and why knowing who created the Snopes family is, in and of itself, more important than knowing who created Snoopy.

It is not that schools merely use such knowledge as a basis for further learning but that all too frequently this kind of knowledge becomes not only the means but the ends of education. From grade school through graduate school we challenge the student to become a trivia expert. Classroom tests, Regents examinations, College Board Scholastic Aptitude Tests, the Princeton Graduate Record Examination—all of these make widespread use of trivia as a basis for judging student learning and aptitude.

And the saddest part is that the students do learn: they learn how to use various study guides—Monarch Notes, Barron's Study Guides, the Made Simple series (even, Socrates forgive us, a *Philosophy Made Simple*); they learn how to prepare for specific trivia questions for each class; they learn that the rewards of education are for the Trivia expert and the punishments for those foolish enough to hazard an original thought.

When the student has demonstrated his proficiency at playing Education Trivia, he is invited to participate in the more esoteric and demanding game of Minutiae, sometimes called "specialization" or "doctoral dissertation." In this variation of Trivia, the player attempts to become expert in some one area of study, preferably an area about which few people know or care. One of the best things about this game is that it allows the player a legitimate "out" when asked general trivia questions: "Goethe? Sorry, I'm a Beaumont and Fletcher man myself." As you can see, this is the perfect defense against a charge of ignorance.

In self-defense, I have created my own game of Minutiae called "Barnabe Googe." Strange as it sounds, Barnabe Googe actually was an Elizabethan poet. Since he is neither well known nor widely read, Googe is perfect for playing Minutiae. I am only going to tell you that he had a wicked way with the "fourteener" (two points for identifying that) and that his work is considered quite representative of English poetry between the time of Wyatt and Surrey (one point apiece) and that of Spenser (one point).

At the moment I seem to have Googe more or less to myself, but I fully expect to see any day now a monumental ten-volume study entitled *Barnabe Googe: His Life, Times, Friends, Works, Habits, Influences, Politics, Religion, Philosophy, and Followers.* Actually, I am myself considering writing a monograph on "Our Neglected Elizabethan: Barnabe Googe" and still another entitled "From Greville to Feveral to Googe." This last should be an important contribution to the Literary Criticism Trivia Game.

John Dewey once wrote, "Education is what is left after the facts are forgotten." Unfortunately, most of what is called education today is concerned more with forgettable facts than with consequential learning. So much time and effort are spent on memorizing the "facts" that little or nothing is left after the facts are forgotten. All that remain are the remnants of the game of Trivia.

For some time George Steiner has been challenging the traditional belief that the study of the humanities makes one more humane. Citing the experience of Nazi Germany—camp officials at Buchenwald and Dachau listening to Bach in the morning and gassing men, women, and children in the afternoon, the Führer himself devoted to Beethoven and Wagner—Steiner calls into question the entire rationale behind the teaching of the humanities.

Actually, it may well be that one of the reasons the teaching of the humanities fails to make us more humane is the manner of the teaching. Go into any art gallery or museum and watch the joy and satisfaction displayed by people if they are able to identify a painting, usually by naming the artist. That a particular painting is by Rembrandt, Van Gogh, Pollock, or Norman Rockwell is less important than the response it evokes in the perceiver. It is the labeling, not the perception, that is the stuff of which art-appreciation classes are made.

In similar fashion, the most common response to music is one of identification, of labeling; whether it be a symphony by Beethoven, an opera by Verdi, or a song by the Beatles it is the labeling that triumphs over the response. It must be noted, however, that the identification of a Beethoven symphony or a Verdi opera has more importance in formal "education" that that of a Beatles song, which only further illustrates the capriciousness of Education Trivia. There is an old joke about a woman who listens to a recording, then reads the album cover and exclaims, "Oh, it was the *Eroica!* That's my favorite symphony!" This is what comes of placing labels before responses—from choosing the letter over the spirit.

I am reminded of a story told to me some years ago by a teacher. It seems that once upon a time there lived a successful clothing manufacturer who had bought a house in Westchester. As a successful man, he felt that he needed a house to mirror his success. Accordingly he had built in the house a library and a hi-fi room fitted with the latest and most expensive audio equipment. All that he lacked was record albums. To remedy this situation, he purchased nineteen feet of record albums—to fill the nineteen feet of space on the shelves of his record library.

Those of us who are tempted to smile superciliously or to laugh aloud at the gaucherie of the clothing manufacturer would do well to examine our own consciences and library shelves. Do you own a set of the Harvard Five-Foot Shelf? Do you participate in the Great Books Game? How about the Book-of-the-Month-Club Game? The Columbia Record Club Game? Have you joined the Metropolitan Museum of Art Seminars in the Home Game?

The clothing manufacturer and the college professor are not different in kind, merely in degree. Both conceive of education as a "matching" process instead of a "making" process. Both are collectors of culture; each places a premium on the amount of labels one is capable of storing. Each is more interested in cataloguing than in creating. The art teacher who flashes two hundred slides on a screen for a student identification test of art; the music teacher who asks questions like "What instruments represent Peter, the Wolf, the grandfather, and the hunters in 'Peter and the Wolf'?"; the literature teacher who requires his students to recognize quotations from ten novels read during the term; the philosophy teacher who asks not "Why?" but "Who wrote?" about the Allegory of the Cave—each of these, and all teachers like them, are engaged not in education (in Dewey's terms) but in Trivia.

Dylan Thomas once wrote of receiving at Christmas "books that told me everything about the wasp, except why." In our schools and universities students learn everything about science, everything about history, everything about philosophy, everything about music and art and literature and life—everything *about* but little or nothing of *why.*

Edwin Land, the inventor of the Polaroid-Land camera, once asked a vital question of educators: "Where, anywhere in life, is a person given this curious sequence of prepared talks and prepared questions, to which the answers are already known?" If I may be permitted a personal definition of Trivia it is that *Trivia consists of asking questions to which the answers are already known.* And what better describes the process of education? So long as we continue to ask students to match instead of make, so long as we continue to be more interested in what and who, in when and where instead of in why, education will remain largely a Trivia contest.

As long as education remains a game of Trivia, I do wish those who plan curricula would open the field up a bit, allowing me to display my erudition in regard to Jimmy Cagney movies, pre-1950 comic books, and the film appearances of Vera Hruba Ralston. In this wish I betray my brotherhood with most educators: I want to play Trivia in the categories I know best.

Of course, there is the possibility—a seemingly absurd one, I grant—that the language of education can be changed into something other than the language of Trivia, into something that will remain long after the facts are forgotten. At the moment, all that is left are the rules of the Trivia Game instead of the important, the consequential, the essential. When the language of education concerns itself with questions to which the answers are not known, with techniques and strategies for survival, in short, with the *why* instead of the *who* and *what* and *when* of education, then, and only then, will education cease to be the greatest Trivia Game in America.

A final note on the Trivia questions in this article: those of you who feel uncomfortable about not knowing the answers to any of the trivia herein have missed the point of my argument and illustrate the validity of my comparison. By the way, whatever happened to Abner Bibberman?

The Language of Educational Research

Alan Shapiro

The results of three recent educational research projects enable one with confidence to talk sense to the American teacher now in the contemporary world of today.

In the first, one group of students was given systematic and direct instruction in dialect variation on Tristan da Cunha Island. The other group was given systematic but indirect instruction in place geography through folk-rock songs which contain the names of American cities. The Tristan da Cunha group was given the option of chewing gum. The place geography group, however, was required to come to class with well-sharpened pencils. The statistically significant results demonstrate that 10 percent of all students lose their hearing by the third grade. The other 90 percent learn to acquire a pronounced left-ear dominance.

The second experiment matched a traditional low-breasted female teacher who is an expert in noun clauses with a bald hump-backed male instructor who believes in the domino theory. Each teacher was asked to apply Northrup Frye's mythic analysis of literary types either to *Silas Marner* or *The Naked Lunch*. The Thematic Apperception Test later administered to a normal group of tenth-graders showed that *The Naked Lunch* students were quieter in the school cafeteria.

The third and most significant experiment called upon four students who were unable to master the "ie" spelling rule to masturbate at least three times a week in the privacy of their home bathrooms. Another set of four students read *Crime and Punishment* while being subjected to strobe lights, overlapping film shots, and the simultaneous and continuous playing of three Bob Dylan records. Chi co-variance factor analysis showed that the students who had been required to mastur-

114

bate enjoyed themselves more than the readers of Dos-
toyevsky.

I have offered these results not because I want to be a
wise-ass but because they demonstrate that we now have at
our disposal research findings which bid fair to revolutionize
American education and because many students across this
broad land hunger for the kind of leadership which these
findings now possibilitize.

The Language of Literary Criticism: Education Meets the Challenge

NAME _____ DATE _____

TITLE _____ AUTHOR _____

PUBLISHER _____ WHERE PUBLISHED _____ WHEN PUBLISHED _____

Who is the subject of this biography? _____

What is the author's purpose in writing this biography? _____

Where did the author get his information—books, magazines, papers, diaries? _____

*EARLY LIFE** List briefly the influences in the subject's early life that helped formulate his personality and developed his talents. Tell briefly some early manifestations that might have been indications of his later success. _____

*SUCCESSES AND FAILURES** Describe briefly the major accomplishments of the person, mentioning the major struggles and failures he encountered. _____

*LATER LIFE** Describe the subject's last years. Were they spent in fame, comfort, obscurity, new work? _____

*PERSONAL QUALITIES** Comment on the subject's personality. _____

*AUTHOR'S TREATMENT** What central idea about the subject does the author try to get across to the reader? _____

Is the author fair and accurate? _____

Summarize the author's opinion of the person. _____

*PERSONAL REACTION**   Why did you like or dislike the book?
_____

Would you like to read more of this author's work or other authors
on the same subject? _____
_____

Do you believe someone reading this biography two or three generations from now would get a true picture of the subject? _____
Explain your answer. _____
_____

—New York City Junior High School

Insights from the Academy

On Linguistic Minting

"One way to make up a word is to coin it."

—Jack E. Conner, *A Grammar of Standard English*

On Defining

"A thing is, literally, anything. Whatever is a center of attention to anyone—to any conscious mind—is a thing. . . .

—Jack E. Conner, *A Grammar of Standard English*

On the Search for Relevance

"I want to make a special point of the fact that whatever is novel in the rhetorical principles advanced in these essays is based on close inductive study of contemporary American prose. . . . The most lucky find, the most radical insight to emerge from this inductive study, prompts the suggestion that our faith in the subordinate clause and the complex sentence is misplaced, that we should concentrate instead on the sentence modifiers, or free modifiers."

—Francis Christensen, *Notes Toward a New Rhetoric*

On Symbol-mindedness

"The importance of word-order in Modern English is easily shown. 'The boy loves the girl' certainly doesn't mean the same as 'the girl loves the boy.' The relative positions of 'the boy' and 'the girl' in this sentence tell us which one is doing the loving; *we have no other way of knowing, because there are no other signals to tell us.*" (Emphasis ours.)

—Joseph H. Friend, *An Introduction to English Linguistics*

The Language of Economics

Robert Lekachman

Economics is an extremely technical subject which, one important specialty aside, deploys a vocabulary drawn mostly from ordinary language, a circumstance which tends to set the economist off from many other specialists. No untrained person is likely to be astonished by his inability to read a page of scientific, medical, or legal writing, for such pages are strewn with words from languages invented to serve the special needs of scientists, doctors, and lawyers. The virtues of good technical language include notational shorthand and precision of communication. Effective technical terms are deliberately shorn of confusing connotation. Literary language, on the contrary, gains richness and loses precision from the connotations which surround the merely denotative. Where economics has come to resemble applied mathematics, econometricians and mathematical economists tend to use a separate, constructed language just like their scientific brethren. Although there is no doubt that the mathematical economists are gaining ground over their literary colleagues, much of economics continues to be written in apparently plain English, even when it is designed for professional use or the instruction of the young.

Consider this bit of exposition:

> What elements constituted aggregate demand? What determined its size and therefore the size of employment and income? Keynes started with the simple assumption that the government had a neutral impact upon the economy. He assumed initially that the government removed as much from the stream of national income in the shape of taxes as it placed in the income stream in the form of its own expenditures on materials and labor services. If the net effect of government operations was zero, the two remaining sources of the aggregate demand for goods and services were consumers and investors.[1]

[1] Robert Lekachman, *The Age of Keynes,* New York, Random House, 1966, p. 91.

The six sentences contain not a single word unknown to an ordinary reader innocent of economic training. Yet the language, standing alone, can scarcely fail to mislead or possibly baffle. The explanation is a clue to the characteristics of plain economic language.

To begin with, the commonplace words are used in special senses. "Aggregate demand," "national income," and "investors" demand specific definition. One does not intuitively realize that aggregate demand is the sum of consumer, investor, and government purchases in a designated geographical area, during a limited period of time, or that national income is a sum of the earnings of the factors of production. And when one is brought to appreciate such definitions, they are likely to push the puzzle further back into questions about what "earnings" and "factors of production" are supposed to mean. Again, the good, honest, greedy soul who buys common stocks in the hope of wealth may think that he is an investor. The economist denies him the title. *Our* investors are businessmen who put up buildings, purchase tools and equipment, or add to their inventories of raw materials or finished goods. The dabbler in common stocks does no more than shift some of his cash into securities at the same time as the person from whom he bought the stock increased his cash holdings and diminished the size of his stock ownership. At the end of the operation there is just as much stock and just as much cash as at the transaction's initiation.

This is only the half of it. In point of fact, it is impossible to grasp this and thousands of similar sober passages[2] without first grappling with the logical structure of the theory which generates the special meanings of everyday words. Full comprehension, it turns out, demands nothing less than insight into the modern, Keynesian theory of income determination. Exposition of the entire theory was the major purpose of the book from which the passage was excerpted. This theory is a series of relationships among economic magnitudes; a kit

[2] I picked this one only because I can reasonably claim to comment authoritatively upon its author's intentions.

of rules to explain the behavior of businessmen who invest, individuals who consume, and governments which run deficits or surpluses; and a set of definitions of the important actors and concepts.

Or reflect upon a second example. In November 1967 England devalued its currency. Worth $2.80 one day, the pound suddenly fell in price to $2.40 the next day, a decline of 14.3 percent. Suppose one commented upon the phenomenon in the economist's typical manner. Here is a constructed comment:

> Devaluation will improve the British balance of payments only if three conditions are met. The elasticity of demand for British exports in general must exceed unity. Where British exporters are selling specific goods whose elasticity of demand in foreign markets exceeds "1," they must reduce prices. Finally, it is essential that British wages do not rise so rapidly as to force export prices up and thus wipe out the possible benefits of devaluation. For devaluation to succeed, then, unemployment rates in Britain should rise moderately so as to discourage trade-union demands for higher wages. Some decline in domestic consumption is probably unavoidable in the short run because of the adverse turn in the terms of trade which is the consequence of any devaluation.

Although I have made the passage up, I can testify to its economic verisimilitude. Suppose we now translate and see what we can derive from the exercise. Here is a free rendering:

> If price cuts on British exports don't attract enough new customers, devaluation is a mistaken policy. Or to put it a bit more exactly, unless a 10 percent price cut attracts rather more than 10 percent new trade, the whole policy is an expensive error. Such is the rule for exports in general. Some exports such as Scotch whisky and Scottish kilts are supported by tastes sufficiently strong and confirmed so that price cuts may attract few additional customers. Men who like bourbon are unlikely to switch to Scotch. However, other exports are directly competitive with American products and here price is an important influence on sales. In such cases, British exporters ought to cut their prices, but whether they can do so depends a good deal on what happens to British wages.

There is only one sure way of keeping British wages low: this is to nudge unemployment high enough so that British unions go easy in their wage demands. But in any eventuality, some British prices must rise because England uses so many imported materials and foodstuffs. These will now be more expensive. If prices rise faster than wages, then the living standards of ordinary Britons will fall. This will be toughest on the poor and the unemployed, but it can't be helped.

Let us see where we are now. The expression "terms of trade," which adorns the last sentence of the untranslated comment, is the ratio of export to import prices. When the prices of the things you export are high and the prices of the things you import are low, what must happen is this: you are able to trade relatively small amounts of your own goods for relatively large quantities of foreign goods. But if you devalue your currency, then your export prices tend to fall and your import prices surely rise. Hence you must now give the foreigners more of your goods in return for the same quantity of theirs and when this occurs all the citizens of the devaluing country must either work harder and produce more in order to maintain the existing level of imports or content themselves with fewer foreign goods. Either way the general standard of life drops. People have either less leisure or fewer goods. Devaluation makes a country poorer right now. Whether after a lapse of time it will release the forces required to make it richer later is another set of issues. And just to make matters worse, before a devaluing nation can be sure that it will even get the chance to work harder for the same results or equally hard for smaller results, its government must be sufficiently beastly to its own working population as to put them in a compliant enough frame of mind to accept a cut in their real earnings.

Was there any reason to guess what the original passage really meant? I should think not. The passage exemplified another characteristic of the economic vocabulary, its ability to disguise the impact upon ordinary humans of specific economic actions. This is rather more than the predictable confusion of the untutored before the conversation of the expert. The economist himself tends innocently to concentrate upon concept and analysis, and to neglect the human effects of his reasoning. The language of economics is conscientiously nonemotive, admirably conceived to lead its users to separate the exercise of their skill from its consequences.

The charge is serious enough to deserve some support from evidence. Here is one important, recent instance of the way economists approach problems of public policy. In the summer of 1967, three eminent economists circulated among their university colleagues a statement on fiscal policy which they were proposing to forward to the House Ways and Means Committee. The document was very carefully worded so as to commit its signers to the support of President Johnson's tax-surcharge proposal but not to his Vietnam policy. The statement argued a technical case. As its authors analyzed the level of military spending, the likely behavior of consumers and investors, and the scale of domestic needs, they foresaw an acceleration in price increases, unless something was done to reduce one of the spending pressures. Raising personal income taxes tends to reduce consumer spending. Hence, ran the analysis, whether or not one supported the Vietnam war, any economist who is opposed to inflation (as all economists are supposed to be by nature) should sign this statement.

In response several hundred economists of varying fame signed, and the statement was duly presented to Congressman Wilbur Mills, who at this writing has chosen to ignore it and similar representations from Administration figures like the Secretary of the Treasury. Here we should pause. Many of the signers did and no doubt continue to oppose American Vietnam involvement and still more the escalation of that involvement. Others did and do support present policy. Why isn't it considered odd, something to be explained, that both groups found it possible to support a tax increase made necessary entirely by the expanding scale of Asian war? Worse still from the standpoint of the assenting doves, passage of the measure would smooth the way for future escalation and be converted by a skillful President into a Congressional expression of support for his military policies. How can a sophisticated citizen, a man of learning and insight, a skilled professional worker, ignore the political causes and consequences of a public policy which happens to fall within his field of specialization?

Apparently quite easily. Does an industrial chemist often inquire whether the drugs he helps to design are overpriced, inadequate, or spuriously advertised? Does a dentist ever wonder whether the Mafia jaw which he makes more comfortable really should improve the happiness of so anti-social a type? Do accountants in the solitary stretches of the night ponder the social value of the companies whose books they audit in the light of day? In each instance the expert's allegiance is to the professional standards of his craft and an ethic which extends no further than honest exercise of skill. So it is, no doubt, with the economist. Because he is appropriately trained, he can gravely pronounce upon inflation and deflation, balance-of-payments deficits and surpluses, and employment and unemployment. But on matters of high foreign and military policy, his position is no stronger than that of the ordinary citizen. His training instructs him not to speak on such matters *as an economist.* The consequence of the self-restraint for the economist is an improvement in his own scientific self-image, his capacity to identify himself with the tradition of the natural sciences. Unhappily there is another effect: by silence a learned profession gives, as Communists used to say, "objective" consent, even to policies of which the economist in his private person disapproves.

The three characteristics of economic language which produce the results so far described are Abstraction, Aggregation, and Impartiality. We might just as well conclude this lament upon the idiotic political consequences of social science by a few comments under each heading.

Abstraction

The plain tongue of economics turns out to be profuse in abstract nouns and passive verbs. The economist rarely talks about a list of actual businessmen who buy specific tools, install them in actual factories, and operate the factories in existing towns and cities. The economist is far more likely to analyze gross private domestic investment. The difference is not trivial. Talk about actual people with actual plans, and the remark that investment is falling is suddenly emotive. Certain men have lost heart. They have reduced their investment plans and fired a certain number of other real people. Shift the conversation to gross private domestic investment and no one need think about anyone in particular or even people in general. Consumer spending is an abstract magnitude apparently unconnected with the spending plans and habits of friends and neighbors. Abstraction in economics, as elsewhere, is the enemy of emotion, the foe of involvement, and, of course, the ally of dispassionate analysis—that jewel to be plucked from the messy data of the real world.

Aggregation

The universe for grown-ups as for infants is one big, buzzing confusion. No man can talk in any orderly way of the multitudinous particulars of social existence. Computers classify and human beings simplify. Aggregation is the economist's favorite mode of simplification. Although he cannot examine the personal history of each unemployed man and woman, he can measure the rate of unemployment and say that 3.8 percent unemployment is to be preferred to 4.1 percent unemployment, as indeed it is. But aggregation like abstraction, its close friend, promotes calm and complacency about the fate of individuals. Labor-market experts know that Negro unemployment runs twice as high as white, and that unemployment rates among Negro teenagers range upward to 35 or 40 percent. This is still not the same as visiting those solid blocks in the Harlems of the big northern cities where during the day the streets are filled with apparently unemployed males, the more active of them hustling, and the less energetic simply filling time as best they can.

What is true of unemployment is equally true of poverty. Aggregates soften suffering and distance emotion. Poverty becomes a percentage of the population whose family income falls below $3300 with adjustments for families larger than four persons. There is comfort to be found in the fact that this percentage has been shrinking. But the urgency of sharp acceleration of present rates of progress is more than trivially diminished by the fact that the poor are a faceless horde of the elderly, Negro, unwed mothers, and dwellers in rural enclaves. The sober music of statistics helps drown out the echoes of suffering.

Statistics are substitutes for observation which is always of particulars. Somehow when the statistician has finished adding up the particulars, the human dimension is subtracted. It is akin to the difference between stabbing one Vietcong with a bayonet propelled by one's own hand and releasing a B-52 bombload on a countryside peopled with a meaningless aggregate, tiny figures scurrying about thousands of feet below one's plane.

Impartiality

Astronomers are neutral about the merits of the stars and the planets. It is a neutrality which separates them from their scandalous relatives, the astrologers. From Newton onward, physicists have dealt with the laws of motion without attention to their human meanings for fear that the laws would favor Englishmen over Frenchmen, poor man over rich, Church of England over Church of Rome. The noble impartiality which is appropriate to the study of the natural universe is the model which has for a long time attracted economists. Lord Robbins' famous three-decades-old definition of the subject heralds economics as the study of the allocation of scarce resources among ends which are unlimited in number. For economists this is an attractive definition, neat, clean, and technically sharp. Moreover, it is wonderfully general. The definition applies to ordinary people trying to get what satisfactions they can out of limited incomes. It speaks to the heart of the businessman's problem of rational expenditure of his resources and borrowings. Naturally it is easily applicable to the budgetary problems of state and federal officials, who must choose among the possible ways of spending what taxes the citizenry will part with short of mutiny.

As an economist, the modern social scientist trumpets his neutrality about the comparative value of personal or public choices. A Galbraith is an unpopular rarity among his fellows. Give the ordinary economist a problem—he will tell you how to analyze it so as to produce a consequence close to the owner of the problem's desire. Several seconds of reflection are enough to perceive what this attitude neglects. What vanishes from attention, *inter alia,* is:

> All concern with the equity of the present distribu-
> tion of income and wealth;
> All consideration of the role of political and social
> power in collecting and exploiting economic resources;
> All serious discussion of the serious objectives of
> resource use.

When the economist takes as given, simply as data of analysis, the pattern of property ownership, the objectives of government, and the choices of spending units, he may think that he is being no more than scientifically neutral. In fact he tacitly endorses the society whose rules he heeds.

Economic language—abstract, aggregative, and impartial—flowers in the work of national income accounting. The profession has taught the rest of the Free World, and apparently the Communists as well, that national progress is to be measured by a single, simple-minded standard—the rate of growth of the Gross National Product. The senselessness of this measure is easy to illustrate. When Detroit increases auto output by a million cars and trucks, GNP rises. Right? Of course. But so does air pollution and in its wake increased medical bills, cleaning bills, and pollution-control devices, all of which also increase GNP. Cigarette production increases GNP and so does the medical treatment of lung cancer. And then the crowning absurdity: war and defense spending increase GNP. Want more "growth"? Just increase the size of the Vietnam war.

The thrust of economics is to avoid as unscientific comparisons between persons and personal goals. Thus it is that although many economists hold strong opinions about the quality of the society in which they live and work, as economists their language, and, therefore, their whole cast of mind, urges them toward the sort of careful, limited analysis of small quantitative problems which by taking for granted what exists ends by silently endorsing the status quo. Since economists feed their metaphors into public discussion, their linguistic biases imperceptibly intrude themselves and so produce a generally conservative vision of society.

When I think that a long time ago I studied economics because I thought it would help me change the world, I feel a vast depression of spirit, possibly consistent with the reputation of my subject.

". . . It's just that the quotation is lower."

James M. Ullman

"Sir, what can I do," the young customer's man asked the veteran stockbroker, "when the market declines and, worse still, the price of a stock I have recommended to my customers goes down with it?"

"Well, now," the old stockbroker said, lighting a cigar and bringing his facile mind to bear on this problem, "don't be discouraged. The fact is, a declining market presents your best opportunity to use the language of stocks."

"Language of stocks?"

"Exactly. When stocks are falling, we have words and phrases calculated to put investors at ease. Indeed, if you are expert, you may even manage to convince an investor that what apparently is bad news actually is good news."

"I don't doubt your assertion for a moment," the young customer's man said cautiously, "but, for instance, what could I have done this morning? An angry man called to complain that his five-thousand-dollar investment, made upon my advice, had declined to one worth not more than four?"

"In that case," the old broker said, "begin by telling the man that the value of his stock is still the same, it's just that the quotation is lower. Then note that the stock in question has what we call built-in value, which is not destroyed by day-to-day fluctuations. Add that the stock is merely consolidating its position, a development that should occasion no alarm."

"I must remember that."

"Don't stop there. Explain further that the temporary decline in the stock's price has brought about an unprecedented opportunity to dollar average. The lower the man's stock goes, you see, the greater his potential for future wealth since he can now buy more shares for the same sum he paid before. This will bring the average per-share cost down; it will accelerate his profits when the price rises again, provided he takes advantage of his good fortune by buying more stock at the depressed level."

"Very good," the young customer's man admitted. "But, sir, what if his thinking is negatively influenced, as is the thinking of so many investors, by the market's overall downward trend, temporary though it may be?"

"Ah, then," the old broker exclaimed, warming to this subject, one very dear to him, "tell him the current decline means that stocks are passing into stronger hands. Weak holders are being shaken out. The implication is that when the selling flurry ends, the only people left holding stocks will be shrewd investors like himself. You might also add—it never does any harm—that tax selling is undoubtedly another underlying factor."

"If the market has been in decline for some time," the customer's man ventured, "some of the more insecure investors may fail to appreciate the reasonableness of this assessment."

"Tell them, then," the old broker advised, "that bargain hunters are moving into the market and the stage is being set for the traditional rally—spring rally, summer rally, year-end rally, or what have you. There is hardly a month in the year when one traditional rally or another is not in the offing."

"An excellent suggestion," the young customer's man replied. "And I am sure it will prove an effective procedure under most circumstances. However, when the Dow-Jones industrial average dropped more than nine points the other day, I was deluged with calls from investors frightened by the unusual steepness of the decline. What reassurances could I have offered?"

"On such a day," the old broker said, "explain to your investors that what is going on may well be what we call a selling climax, an event professionals have been awaiting with anticipation, since it will signal the end of the market's bearish phase. The more precipitate the day's decline, in fact, the more likely that the bullish rebound to follow will be vigorous and prolonged. And so once again what apparently is bad news becomes, to the informed investor, the best of all possible news."

"I think I understand now the approach you advocate," the young customer's man said, "and I must confess I admire its subtle simplicity. A final question. During a declining market, I may be introduced to potential customers. How do I get them enthused about stocks when the averages are falling and the boardroom is permeated with gloom?"

"Very easily," the old broker replied. "You emphasize to these people—and to anyone else who might inquire—that the current market is *selective*."

"Selective?"

"Yes. By that we mean some stocks will go up in price, and some will go down. You can readily demonstrate the truth of this because even on the worst days, when the average tumbles twelve points or so, there are always a few stocks going up."

"I see. You thus imply that one cannot buy just any stock

and expect to get rich. But you hint that, irrespective of what the majority of stocks are doing, the informed and intelligent investor, in which class your potential client undoubtedly falls, can profit by buying those stocks which will rise nevertheless."

"Precisely," the old broker beamed. "Moreover, the word also suggests that wise hands like yourself may even know the identities of these rising stocks."

"But what," the young customer's man asked, "if I have absolutely no idea as to which stocks will rise?"

"That doesn't matter," the old broker concluded. "The main thing is that people *think* you have. Or that someone somewhere has. Investor confidence, you see, is the mainstay of our business."

The Language of Love
Wanted: Ways of Saying It

Max Weatherly

"Before they lead me into that little square room tomorrow, Miss Tittywopp, I gotta tell ya something."

"Yes, Monroe?" It was the grillwork between teacher and student that made it possible to hold back tears: it represented a certain pattern of action beyond which she felt she shouldn't go; it was necessary dignity.

"My last thoughts'll be of you." He searched her face for the expected, the needed, tears. "I've always loved you, Miss Tittywopp."

Inundation. The grillwork liquefied and disappeared. "Why didn't you tell me," sobbing, "Monroe?"

"I reckon it was that old nonverbal syndrome." Sigh. "Hayakawa says we think one way, act another way, and talk yet another way. Semantic gap, maybe. I reckon holding up that filling station and knocking that guy off was a realization growing out of early erotic frustrations. I didn't actually *want to,* you see. I wanted to insert my male member in its erected state into your sweet little vaginal canal and tell you that way. I—"

"Oh, Monroe, I wanted to cook for you and make you happy. You could have stuck your—your finger in my eye if you'd wanted to. Oh, oh, oh . . ." All floodgates now open.

"Inadequacies of language, I reckon." He sighed.

Monroe was right. He was right indeed—and the trouble begins, ironically enough, with the word *love.* The ancient Greeks, monuments of sensibility that they were, had three words for love: *eros,* representing the feelings that existed so tragically and vainly between Monroe and his schoolteacher; *filios,* representing the feelings Monroe harbored for his close kin; and *agape,* naming the kind of love he held for his fellow man—the feelings that broke down under some deep-seated strain and opened the way for him to commit the ultimate act of hate.

We modern Americans, monuments of insensibility that we are, tend to simplify *ad absurdum* for what we insanely call "convenience." We have "all-purpose" cleaners, automobiles, foods, vacations and clothing, to mention only a few current simplifiers. We also have far too many all-purpose words—and one of them is *love,* which names an emotion of such infinite variety that it demands the deepest delineation. Due to its myriad uses in all three areas defined by the Greeks, *love,* the modern word, has collected denotations, connotations, and semantic furbelows to such an extent that to my mind it now resembles a swarm of bees "protecting" the queen. And I wonder (when I'm not making love) what we're afraid of? What are we *really* doing in the name of "linguistic convenience"?

In the realm of erotica plain old instinct will get you a long way without a word. In addition there is man's most honest organ, the eye. When I lived in Arabia I learned that Arabs, who take the greatest delight in "outwitting" each other (I'm avoiding the phrase *lying to* out of love for my Arab friends who lie to each other in the Western, or acceptable, manner), depend heavily on what they read in each other's eyes. Over the centuries they have become so adept at this that we Americans, having witnessed breath-taking demonstrations of that ability (and probably having been caught in a couple of breath-taking lies ourselves) either adopted a handful of the devious expressions which Arabs themselves used or stopped, if you can believe it, lying to them. The eye is rather honest and it works as well in love as it does in business. Laying hands on your beloved, for example, you can with only a modicum of perceptiveness tell right away whether or not your attentions are welcomed.

But what do we do for words? I know a man who is so emotionally stimulated by (read "in love with") a woman of our mutual acquaintance that his knees, poor devil, turn to glue the moment he sees her. He becomes so hung-up for appropriate words that he stands slack-shouldered in her presence with the most pained expression upon his face and with his palms nearly dripping. I never know whether to laugh, cry, or just kiss them both and walk away when we meet in the corridors of the university where we teach. She could probably rummage around in her mind and find some make-do words, for she is equally enamored of him. But she is female, as you've already guessed, and is therefore culturally denied the right (read "pleasure") of initiative. So the years go by and they stand gazing at each other like a pair of virgin iguanas.

And the problem isn't merely his shyness: he would be far less shy if there were words at hand which weren't either asinine or "obscene." He has, my friend, too much integrity, too much essential dignity (if you can believe it) to say, "Will you join me for a cup of coffee?" He doesn't want to drink coffee, he wants to make joyous, raunchy, glorious, and patently physical love. He wants to wallow in the Elysian Fields of erotica with his lady love. But there isn't any word for what he wants. Well, there is, but it would alienate her.

Let's suppose he suffers through the cup-of-coffee insanity and they have indeed achieved the threshold of one of their bedrooms by some miracle of communication. What then? She can't (so how does he?) say, "Let's undress and climb on the rack," in an appropriate manner. Of course most people "know." But suppose she doesn't? And, since "knowing" suggests prior experience, is she, culturally shackled hand and foot, apt to demonstrate it? Then what should they say? And, for that matter, how many words should they use? (Who among us has not at one awful time or another talked something to death?) I myself have been in situations where the pantomime became downright ludicrous.

I want to suggest nonpsychological origins of shyness. I say there is no dumbshow dumber than a man and a woman about to enjoy each other's bodies for the first time! I say the language of erotica is, by dismal default, silence.

Filially, our language doesn't stand up much better. Monroe's primary relationship to Miss Tittywopp was, after all, filial. As his schoolteacher she was a parent symbol: That she became anything more was, even if a reason for rejoicing, secondary. Was it, then, any easier for him to stay after school and say, "You are so good to me, Miss Tittywopp. You seem to have my best interests at heart and you seem to want to help me become a better person. I love you"? Indeed it was not! For in classless and sexless America, Miss Tittywopp would in all likelihood have assumed (feared) that her young male charge was making advances.

Poor Monroe might have been able to go home and say to his mother, "I love you." But, depending on the spectrum of her various neuroses, he might also have got his ears boxed. Such a declaration to his father would have been met with indignation or, at best, a hurried visit to the psychiatrist; and, said to his brother, the words would have got him snickered at.

Until they began voting for all the wrong candidates, I very much loved my two older brothers. I'm sure there was a fairly usual amount of erotic love in my feelings, but it was mostly a wish to be like them physically and psychologically—identification, hero worship. But I couldn't even say to my brother Pete, "I hero-worship you." I couldn't even say, "I love you," to my two sisters, whom I indeed loved, each in different ways. Yet I felt love, a certain kind of love, and wanted very much to express it.

There is one beam of light in the filial darkness: one can, reduced by default as I have shown to wordlessness, act out one's love. Why? Because there is time. For better or for worse, we humans spend more time, in the aggregate, with our *filials* than we do with our *eroses* or our *agapes*. And I must say I think there is some validity in acting out one's love as opposed to verbalizing it. My father could not, for his own special reasons, even *like* me. He spent the first twenty-five years of my life acting out that painful fact. Then he arrived at two points in his own life: (1) His last years, and (2) the realization that he had made a tragic mistake. He spent, therefore, his final four years acting out an apology to me; and I spent them trying to act out my forgiveness. I hope we both succeeded, but the fact will never be established. And therein lies the greatest objection to acting out.

The fact remains that we English-speaking peoples need

words badly, appropriate words. I think I'll tack a sign on the front of my house, "WORDS WANTED."

Erotica and filiality are names of important and beloved emotions. But when I compare them to the high, wide and deep inferences of *agape* they recede slightly toward the trivial. Surely there is more human happiness because of, and more human suffering for the lack of, *agape*. If Monroe's *agape* had held up, for instance, he would not have killed the filling-station attendant: the poor man would still be alive, for which at least his wife would be grateful (not to mention his known children) and poor old Monroe would be free to find some way however stumblingly to tell Miss Tittywopp that he loved her.

But we English-speakers (or so we can technically call ourselves) can't go around saying, "I *agape* you," to Tom, Dick, and Jane no matter how close we might happen to be. I once tried such an experiment: I went to my favorite professor one gorgeous spring afternoon determined to speak to him of my gratitude, my devotion and, in short, my *agape*. "Professor Doggyball," I said manfully, "I think you're a great man—I guess I sort of love you." He searched my face in a panic. "Well. Thanks, Weatherly." He managed a most patronizing chuckle. "I'm not sure what my wife'd say about that, but thanks." I departed, my rapport with him in shambles and my ego in shreds. One time a young lawyer my own age did me a legal favor free of charge. When I wrote my thanks I signed the letter (where you would ordinarily put *sincerely* or *cordially*) *agape*. I thought surely my gesture would be understood in view of his youth, but I never heard from him again.

Flower people are doing their dead level best to pound the square word *love* into the round hole *agape*. The word is, joyfully, coming into wider use nowadays—even between men friends in eroticaless situations. As a result of a recent television program, I got a fan letter from a teenager in Connecticut signed, "Love and flowers, Gail Smith." And I thought that was a pretty nifty way of putting it. So maybe there is some hope.

You see, it's *agape* and not *eros* that makes the world go round. That's one thing we Madison Avenue–oriented Americans can't seem to get through the semantic fog emanating from that benighted area. It's *agape* that has made the men of this earth give up cannibalism and slavery, however slowly they have done it. *Agape* has produced great works of art and enriched men's lives. It can even be said to feed on itself and propagate itself in just that way. It could eliminate war, I think, given a fair chance by heavily verbal Greed (e.g., avarice, craving, covetousness, rapacity, voraciousness, gluttony, cupidity, insatiability, and their myriad cousins like mania and rage). But it will never get that chance until there are ways of saying it!

I think I'll tack another sign up on the front of my house, "WANTED:WAYS OF SAYING IT."

I maintain that each of us is being separated from everyone else with the reverse speed of love. It's like the expansion of the solar system but it's more immediate because instead of planets it's people! If we could just say, "Love!" or, "I Love You!" it would seem that perhaps the process could be reversed. The awful outward-going would suddenly become an inward-going and soon we'd be together again and could touch each other and take each other in our arms like *The Catcher in the Rye* and be real human beings again.

And I further say that anything else, any other course, leads to a graveyard, a corporeal and linguistic graveyard. The silly dialogue with which I began writing could be my funeral oration in that linguistic graveyard. Oh, we aren't dead yet, I would have to admit. But if something isn't done our demise isn't very far off, as civilizations are born and killed. And if we are really headed for that great lexicon in the sky, I have a feeling we won't have left behind nearly as interesting a language as did our forebears, the ancient Greeks.

The Silent Languages of Psychotherapy

Norman Mactas Ackerman and
Gary Stuart Burstein

And the whole earth was of one language and of one speech.
. . . And they said, "Come, let us build us a city, and a
tower, with its top in heaven, and let us make us a name,
lest we be scattered abroad upon the face of the whole
earth." . . . And the Lord said, "Behold, they are one people,
and they have all one language, and this is what they begin
to do. . . . Come let us go down, and confound their language that they may not understand one another's speech."
So the Lord scattered them abroad from thence upon the
face of all the earth, and they left off to build the city.
Therefore was the name of it called Babel. . . .

Holy Scripture; Author Unknown

Psyche—a nymph, the personification of the soul and spirit
. . . excited the jealousy and hatred of Venus (goddess of
beauty) who ordered Cupid (god of passion) to inspire
Psyche with love for some contemptible human being.
Instead Cupid himself fell in love with Psyche. After many
persecutions by Venus, a conciliation was affected, and
Psyche was made immortal.

Therapy—to nurse, to cure.

Webster's New Twentieth Century Dictionary

The languages of psychotherapy are numerous: the metalan-
guages of theory; the action languages of the speechless horrors of electric shock therapy, prefrontal lobotomy, and the
hypertranquilizing drugs; the verbal languages of the intellectual gymnasts (orthodox Freudian psychoanalysis, theo-
logical counseling, and the guidance of the social worker); and
the silent languages of psychotherapy, the messages communicated through the life style, the patterns of sleep and
dreams, and the language of the body.

Of all the languages within the psychological tower of Babel,
none are perhaps so loud yet unheard, so obvious yet unno-

ticed as the silent ones. The silent languages of psychotherapy are, like all other languages, compressed and codified experiences communicated over space and time. Like other languages, they are created by man, made meaningful by man, reformed and reshaped by man in response to his needs, perceptions, and reality and the needs and perceptions of his society. And, like all languages created by man, the silent languages give us keys to the nature of their creator. If man is truly "the measure of all things," then the silent and noisy products of the mentally ill are as much the nature of man as are the creations of the most rational thinkers.

To begin, we will enter the psychological tower of Babel concentrating on the silent languages. We will use different styles to translate silence into meaning. We will explore, probe, hypothesize, and contradict in order to open some doors to the understanding of the noisy world of silence.

We have catalogued below ten of the most common myths about psychotherapy, and in contrast have provided brief descriptions of the actual processes to which these myths ostensibly refer.

1. *Mental institutions are created to cure the mentally ill!*

Not so. Unstated in institutional psychotherapy is the fact that the institution must maintain the status quo of society and is therefore incapable of dealing with the aberrations in its midst without resorting to shock therapy, prefrontal lobotomy, and the inevitable use of the hypertranquilizing drugs. Such institutions say by their very existence that there is no cure for the mentally deranged, but that if the patient can be "brainwashed" into repeating and *believing* what is required he will be free to go back into our version of society.

2. *Psychotherapy is a generalized method used for the rehabilitation of the mentally ill!*

Not so. Unstated in the clinical practice of psychotherapy is the fact that each class of society receives its own brand of therapy, which acts to maintain the vested interests of the ruling groups.

3. *The patient and therapist will work together toward a common understanding of health!*

Not so. Rarely in the negotiation for this most precious contract, the psychotherapeutic process, is there a mutual understanding of the desired results of the therapy. In office therapy, the patient approaches therapy as an activity of minimal personal involvement (although a great deal of time and money is spent), wherein a specialist well trained in the lore and rituals of the analytic doctrine will *cause* changes to occur.

4. *The goal of psychoanalysis is that the patient will be able to function in an independent and mature manner after the resolution of his transference to the therapist!*

Not so. It is never made clear that the goal of classical psychoanalysis is the termination of the deep personal relationship between the therapist and the patient. The fact that both the patient and the therapist will strive to regain their noninvolvement status after much time and effort has been expended to creating a vital, functional dialogue between two former strangers is a symptom of the disease of alienation now rampant in our society.

5. *The understanding of the past will lead to personality changes in the present!*

Not so. Unstated in the office practice of psychotherapy is the theoretical understanding that the basic personality cannot be changed, and all that can occur is the removal of an elaboration of symptom reactions; that the emotional understanding of past events does not precipitate behavior changes, but that the adult can never relive and therefore never change the experiences of the child.

6. *The therapist is the therapist and the patient is the patient!*

Not so. Silent are the statistics of the suicide rate among therapists. This rate is many times greater than among the average population, reflecting either the heightened awareness and sensitivity in the healer driving him to the brink, or the degree of buried hostility in the patient which when brought to the surface lashes firstly and consistently at the healing hand.

7. *The unconscious is the great storehouse of the past, of*

which we can catch only a glimpse through dreams, slips of the tongue, and symptoms!

Not so. Silent is the knowledge that the unconscious may not exist, but that all memories may lurk in the recesses of the mind, waiting only for the correctly formulated questions to evoke them.

8. *The patient explores his past and the therapist interprets it by therapy!*

Not so. Perhaps the unstated actuality is closer to the idea of George Orwell if we substitute a few words (in brackets) in this quotation from *1984:*

> The past is whatever the records and the memories agree upon. And since the party [therapist] is in full control of all records, and in equally full control of the minds of its members [patients] it follows that the past is whatever the party [therapist] chooses to make it. Six means eighteen, two plus two equals five, war is peace, freedom is slavery, ignorance is strength.

9. *The therapist analyzes the verbal and intellectual distortions of the patient!*

Not so. Distortions are considered unique to the patient, but we should realize distortions are also due to the therapist's personal and theoretical analytic interpretation. The therapist functions as a simultaneous translator of the pattern of his own voice and prejudice, and the verbal signals of the patient.

10. *Our psychological theories definitively describe man's development and functioning!*

Not so. In mental health today, all is experimentation and exploration, all is trial and error. We can drug, blast, mutilate, soak, dry, touch, listen, feel, smell, and hear but we still do not have the slightest idea of what makes man function. All psychological theories are merely hypotheses, but we too frequently find these hypotheses accepted as facts by therapists and patients alike. A starting point of understanding would be to accept all "facts" as merely hypotheses and to strive toward a descriptive understanding of psychological reality. No thought of man, no matter how wild it seems, must be left unconsidered in the attempt to construct man's psychological model.

The Language of the Functioning Body

More directly conveyed than by spoken words are the messages portrayed by the stance, attitude, motion, gesture, and mannerism of the body, appendages, and face of the individual. As emphasized by the actor-director Stanislavski and by the character analyst Wilhelm Reich, there is an encyclopedic volume of information revealed in the shape and movement of the human body. Here in this shadow play of substance, and in this silent ballet of function, do we find the silent language of the functioning body.

Everyone can recognize the happy face, joyous walk, and swinging arms of the schoolboy on his way to the movies, or the downcast eyes, hunched shoulders, and plodding tread of the same boy after failing a school examination. Books, poems, plays, and art pieces on the one hand, and clinical descriptions, psychiatric theses, and psychological lectures on the other, all describe, demonstrate, and utilize the million and one varieties of mood, expression, or attitude that the functioning body can proclaim.

But, for the sake of brevity, let us consider just one of the most important functional attitudes assumed by man today, an attitude widespread in distribution and dire in prediction which we shall label "turtle-itis."

"Turtle-itis" refers to man's imitation of the turtle. The turtle's natural protective armor against the outside world is a hard, thick, rigid shell. When the turtle becomes frightened, it withdraws its head, legs, and tail into the womblike shell for protection against real or unreal outside threats. The apparent contradiction is of course that at this point of greatest protection the turtle has become completely immobile and most vulnerable to damage. It could starve to death, develop stasis diseases because of nonexercise, or even end up in the cooking pot.

Man resembles the turtle in that his external muscular

structure can act, as does the hard shell of the turtle, as a protective device, as a suit of armor. This rigid muscular stance is intended to prevent or retard the external world from physically or emotionally penetrating to the sensitive inner core of the individual. The muscular suit of armor also bars the vital inner thoughts, feelings, and physiologic expressions from reaching out to the surrounding social and physical environment. The abnormal muscular shell hinders man's ability to be involved in meaningful work, to blend with another in a loving act, or to search for the vital truths of life. Again, like the turtle withdrawn into its shell, the muscular armored man or woman can die of emotional starvation, waste away from nonuse of natural physical responses, or stew in the juices of his own fear and hatred.

The characteristics of the muscular armored man are easy to identify. The face is without changing expression; the eyes are dead, lacking the aliveness and luster so easily seen in the eyes of a healthy child; the mouth is constricted and tight; and the facial muscles are restricted to a single constant expression. One gains the general impression that this person wears a mask as inflexible as the turtle shell.

The upper portion of the body is held in a rigid, immobile position with shoulders chronically tensed and raised to "carry the world"; breathing is drastically curtailed with full expiration virtually impossible, since the chest muscles and diaphragm are tensed, restricting the flexibility needed for deep breathing; back muscles are chronically rigid, functionally expressing unreleased fears and angers; the abdomen is pulled in and cramped; the pelvic area immobile and retracted, preventing full sexual expression from developing in a love embrace.

When does this attitude of turtle-itis first start? It starts moments after birth. It starts as the newborn infant, a live, mobile energy system, faces the real world of the future; an upside-down world punctured by the slap of the deliverer's hand.

From the outset the newborn finds that attempts at physical mobility will be met frequently by the harsh "NO!"

response of the environment. The natural, living, expressive outward movements are reshaped by admonition toward immobility, and the young infant literally and figuratively shrinks from the hostile environment. This withdrawal or shrinking from the environment can begin even while the child lies in the womb of a mother, who suffers from turtle-itis and has a tense, immobile uterus restricting the natural, expansive prenatal growth.

After birth the infant can first learn the loud "NO!" of his environment if he is "untimely ripped" from his mother's warmth and protection and placed in another room "for hygienic reasons"; or he can learn the violent statement of "NO!" when fed through a dead rubber nipple or by a contracted, unliving breast of the rigid mother. The male child may also be subjected to the violent "NO!" of the mutilation of his penis—again, "for hygienic reasons."

Thus, even in the earliest moments of life the child may begin to learn how to erect a barrier between himself and the harsh outside world by tensing his body in preparation for the violent acts he expects from a hostile environment. This body-tensing, this desire to stay rigid, gradually becomes the chronic physical attitude of the child. Here is the shell-like façade which hides the child's true feelings and thoughts from the environment, and which leads to the muscular armor of the fearful, hateful, deadened adult. Here also is the shell-like muscular façade that all of us develop to a greater or lesser degree.

This shell-like muscular façade is the suit of armor that we all wear as our silent proclamation of "NO!" to life. It is a façade that prevents us from ever being involved in a deeply emotional manner in love, or meaningful work, or the pursuit of knowledge. Instead of finding our body a mobile instrument ready for expansive external communication or for contractile protection as the situation demands, we find ourselves sentenced to live within a dark and lonely, rigid shell, which, although it protects us from the outside world, at the same time transforms us into shrinking, immobile, and uncommunicative organisms. How pathetic is man, heir to a million potential physical messages of function but restricted mainly to one joyless, rigid expression of existence.

The Silent Premise: Our Personal Language

Most, if not all, theories of personality development stress the importance of the early years in determining the future growth of the individual; but the question still remains as to *how* such experiences actually affect growth. By what means does the individual carry continuity from the past through the present to the future?

We all need a sense of continuity in our lives, and it is this need that requires us to try to structure our lives in a meaningful way.

One link connecting our various experiences through time we call "conscious thought." When we think, we reflect upon ourselves and, in self-reflection, become aware of our "identity." We look at the past from the point of view of the present—and in doing so form a structure in which the past and present "selves" are now inextricably bound.

But neither "thoughts" nor "memories" are direct experiences of reality. Both processes involve selections from those experiences that constantly bombard our senses, which we codify, organize, categorize, and evaluate, and in some way tag or label by the time-binding medium of language. Language is the primary medium through which man binds time, orders the past, present, and future, and creates for himself an identity, a self-concept.

We have begun to recognize in the patients we meet daily a peculiar use of another silent language, a highly personalized form of logic that results in a life style unique to the individual. In exploring the dynamics of this language-logic, or psycho-logic, with our patients, we have found that at the base of each such personal language is a silent premise used to transform and to fix the changing multidimensional world of experiences into a consistent series of events.

The development of the personal language in early life coincides with the child's acquisition of what, for want of a better term, we will call the "public language"—a learning process occurring in the critical period between the ages of two and four years in the physiologically normal child when the child acquires the ability to distinguish between the external world and his own internal world. At the same time the child acquires the ability through language to select, identify, and mentally codify events for future conscious retrieval. As the child is acquiring the "public language" he also experiences one or more significant social events involving himself and one or more other individuals. This significant social event then becomes a critical, evaluative memory in the developing individual.

Either as a fantasy screen-memory or actual recall of the primal social situation, this earliest memory seems to act like a template for the future social behavior of the individual. As the individual continues to act and react in social circumstances, a pattern of thought, behavior, and feeling develops which we can label the life style of the individual. Self-observation, shaped by the language template, of the life style leads one to form a relatively conscious but unstated hypothesis about life, the silent premise, which further reinforces the functional fixedness of the life style. Thus the silent premise becomes the code by which the individual gauges the stimulus responses of the external world; or, stated differently, the silent premise becomes the perceptual filter by which only those interpretations consistent with the life style of the individual are admitted into conscious thought.

This highly personal language, this silent premise about life, is not a language we normally share with others. It is a language we use to converse with ourselves, to create a monologue of functional or frozen consistency. By exploring the silent premise situation with the patient, we have found time after time that individuals are well aware of their premises about life, but that they do not verbalize them. If a patient is asked to describe the earliest memory which includes at least one other human, he almost always describes a significant event that occurred between the ages of two and four years. By "exploring" this event, the therapist can develop insight into the main silent premise that has formed and re-formed the life style of the patient. If the goal of therapy is to change behavior, then this can at times be accomplished by helping the patient to verbalize this silent premise and so permit a change in his life style.

The Voiceless Languages of Sleep and Dreams

About one third of our existence occurs in the silent shadow world of sleep, replete with nightmares, dreams, and quiescent slumber. This world has teased and vexed the waking imagination of man since the time when primitive man color-rubbed his waking and sleeping fears and dreams on the grey walls of the cave-houses. Each culture has given infinitely varied symbolic labels to the hidden (covert) meanings of dreams/ nightmares based on a finite number of apparent (manifest) objects and activities.

According to Luce and Segal,[1] dreams have been interpreted by the Fiji Islanders as departures of the soul; by the ancient Egyptians as portents of the future; by the early Greeks as means of healing the sick; by the Iroquois Indians as commands to be followed; by the Inquisition judges as reason for death by burning; by religious innovators as the basis for new religions; by Romantic-era writers as the flame for imagination; by modern scientists as the completion of the hypothetical question; by psychoanalysts of all schools as a therapeutic instrument.

Throughout the ages of man, complete civilizations have risen and fallen, cultures have waxed and waned, people have been lauded or destroyed because of dreams and their contents; but today, in our supreme egotism, we moderns feel that only we have the true disclosures about dreams, sleep, and the sleep state. We talk of the modern psychoanalytic interpretation of dreams, or the psychophysiologists' experiments with REM (rapid eye motion) sleep, or the electroencephalographers' interpretation of the sleeping rhythms of the brain as the reality and quintessence of knowledge.

[1] *Sleep,* New York, Coward-McCann, 1966.

As in the over-all psychotherapeutic process, the therapeutic interpretation of the mental productions of the sleep-dream state is a delicate negotiation between the masquerade memories of the patient and the trained intuition of the therapist. The interpretive language of dreams and nightmares is hypothetical, inconclusive, and suggestive and is thought of as conclusive and exact only by fools, frauds, and fanatics. It is a language we have yet to learn.

Quiet Words for the Future

If madness is defined as a deficient alphabet in the languages of life, and if psychotherapy in all its verbal, physical, and silent languages has not ended the ever-growing numbers of people afflicted with madness, then we should be prepared for the advent and dispute of new and varied languages directed toward the cure of the ailing spirit.

The statement that the psychoneurotic and the psychotic may have a greater version of the truth, although they are struck lame, dumb, or blind because of it, may grate upon professionally trained ears.

But, at present, therapy is still a cosmological shell game, with knowledge about which shell you are under practically limited to an educated guess. Man has yet fully to discover and learn the languages of communication, fully to differentiate the form from the function, fully to isolate the monologue from the dialogue.

Electronic-computer-assisted therapy, ESP and mental telepathy, electromagnetic-field phenomena, biochemical-endocrine therapy, social-revolutionary education, genetic-uterine modalities, hypnoidal-state explorations, gestalt signal-maze studies, systems-approach methodology, revisionist psychoanalytic schools, and untold numbers of others with varied degrees of "scientific" validity will emerge in the future to change the language and process of psychotherapy, each with its own template languages.

Editor's Note: No language in America contains more mysteries than the language of psychotherapy. Few languages contain more opportunity for violent, emotional, and personal disagreement than the language of psychotherapy. That is the reason that we invited not one but three (or two, if you count collaborators Ackerman and Burstein as one) commentators to examine it. Our thought was that Drs. Ackerman and Burstein would advance their thesis and Dr. Kaplan would write a rejoinder. Instead, as might have been predicted, what follows is what happened.

Rejoinder

To the Editors:

I am returning the manuscript of Drs. Ackerman and Burstein, which I managed to get through only out of morbid curiosity. Drivel is what the good doctors have presented you with. And I might interject, incidentally, that they have played beanbag with the organization of their paper. This and the abominable writing leave the paper unsuitable, in my opinion, for any sort of publication, save possibly its being mimeographed and distributed among those of my profession now gravitating toward Big Sur, hairy neanderthals who cannot read without a forefinger inching across the text and moving lips.

You suggest a rebuttal? A rebuttal is inappropriate. For what we have here is no argument but a *shtick,* as we used to say in vaudeville, an antic, a bit, a thing. And it goes something like this:

The psychotherapeutic situation evokes many variables. Which variables the doctor uses to perform therapy is a function of that doctor's relationship to the professional Establishment. Since the ideology of any Establishment is conservative, those doctors who identify with the Establishment will use only those variables in the psychotherapeutic situation which guarantee that the patient will not change. Since most doctors are closely related to the Establishment, most psychotherapy operates with the wrong variables. Thus the patient is deluded about the service he is paying for—the patient wants to change, you see, but his doctor won't allow this because this threatens the doctor's vested interests. To make matters worse, the therapist himself is unaware of all this, inasmuch as he has been indoctrinated into paying attention to the wrong variables. Most therapists are naïve, yet diabolical, fools.

Enter Drs. Ackerman and Burstein. They are on to the truly effective variables—"the silent languages of psychotherapy." How did they come upon these secrets? They have listened to their patients communicate through means wholly unexpected in "normal" society. Their patients say things with their bodies—by gesture and posture—and with connotative resonances of language.

Now, not only don't other practitioners realize this, but the Establishment, in not realizing this, has constructed a theoretical system of mind with a fraudulent explanatory power. This is Act I.

Act II consists of introducing alternative terminology having a greater explanatory power. Never mind the Establishment concept of "defense mechanism." "Turtle-itis" really explains the patient's problem. Moreover, the entire approach to the functioning of memory is wrong, as is the etiologic concept of psychopathology. We are all sick. Civilization is a plague. Can't you see that?

Act III establishes the qualifications for judging Acts I and II. Your disagreement defines you as part of the Establishment. Hence you are disqualified to judge the merits of Acts I and II.

The fact is that the whole *shtick* is based on misrepresentation of the actual state of affairs, conceptually, theoretically, and technically. For example, there is no variable mentioned by these two doctors that is not a subject of responsible research at this very moment. As for the relationship between body and mind, this dichotomy is one of the most grisly philosophic problems, something these two ignoramuses fail to appreciate, and it requires painstaking labor to comprehend the articulation of body and mind. René Spitz, for example, has devoted his life to the study of the problem. The late Felix

Deutsch tried his hand at it. Richard Yazmajian of Downstate Medical is working on the problem—and this is to mention only three of hundreds. Whereas the Messiah (like that third-rate fanatic Wilhelm Reich) can mix metaphors, leap from abstract to concretistic thinking without specifying transformation rules, reputable workers on these problems respect the complexity of the undertaking and so appear less spectacular and sensational. I won't go into the problem of memory, for I get dizzy merely thinking about it. Yet, the Messiah has solved it all.

Nor is it much of a scoop to discover that a good theory in the hands of a jackass results in a poor product. There are, to be sure, many jackasses. Drs. Ackerman and Burstein would have us scrap the theory. This would be like destroying a Mozart symphony because several orchestras are giving bad performances.

I tell you this isn't even a good *shtick*. I can't imagine anyone taking this seriously. A few readers perhaps will enjoy the noise of disruption this pap—this compost—makes. But that's all.

I am awfully sorry I couldn't have something nicer to say about something submitted to you.

Do we have room for a little Santayana?

> Masks are arrested expressions and admirable echoes of feelings, at once faithful, discreet and superlative. Living things in contact with the air must acquire a cuticle, and it is not urged against cuticles that they are not hearts; yet some philosophers seem to be angry with images for not being things, and with words for not being feelings. Words and images are like shells, no less integral parts of nature than are the substances they cover, but better addressed to the eye and more open to observation. I would not say that substance exists for the sake of appearance, or faces for the sake of masks, or the passions for the sake of poetry and virtue. Nothing arises in nature for the sake of anything else; all these phases and products are involved equally in the round of existence . . .

You see the tone? The respect, the dignity? Compare that to the Messiah's tone.

Best regards,
Donald Kaplan

The Language of Psychotherapy
(Circa 1688)

Excerpts from *Recorded Observations of Witchcraft* by Cotton Mather

It was the eldest of these children that fell chiefly under my own observation; for I took her home to my own family, partly out of compassion to her parents, but chiefly that I might be a critical eyewitness of things that would enable me to confute the Sadducism of this debauched age. Here she continued well for some days, applying herself to actions of industry and piety. But on Nov. 20, 1688, she cried out, *Ah, they have found me out!* and immediately she fell into her fits; wherein we often observed she would cough up a ball as big as a small egg, into the side of her windpipe, that would near choke her till by stroking and by drinking it was again carried down.

When I prayed in the room, first her hands were with a *strong,* though not *even,* force clapt upon her ears; and when her hands were by our force pulled away, she cried out, *They make such a noise, I cannot hear a word!* She complained that *Glover's* Chain was upon her leg; and assaying to go, her gait was exactly such as the *chained witch* had before she died. When her tortures passed over, still frolics would succeed, wherein she would continue *hours,* yea, *days* together, talking perhaps never wickedly but always *wittily* beyond herself; and at certain provocations her torments would renew upon her, till we had left off to give them; yet she frequently told us in these frolics, *that if she might but steal or be drunk, she would be well immediately.* She told us *that she must go down to the bottom of our well* (and we had much ado to hinder it) *for they said there was plate there, and they would bring her up safely again.*

We wondered at this, for she had never heard of any plate there; and we ourselves, who had newly bought the house were ignorant of it; but the former owner of the house just then coming in, told us *there had been plate for many years lost at the bottom of the well.* Moreover, one singular passion that frequently attended her was this:

An *invisible chain* would be clapt about her, and she in much pain and fear, cry out when *they* began to pull on it. Sometimes we could with our hands knock it off, as it began to be fastened; but ordinarily, when it was on, she would be pulled out of her seat with such violence, towards the fire, that it was as much as one or two of us could do to keep her out. Her eyes were not brought to be perpendicular to her feet when she rose out of her seat, as the mechanism of the human body requires in them that rise; but she was dragged wholly by other hands. And if we stamped on the hearth just between her and the fire, she screamed out *that by jarring the chain, we hurt her.*

I may add that *they* put an unseen rope, with a cruel noose, about her neck, whereby she choked until she was black in the face, and though it was got off before it had killed her, yet there were the red marks of it, and of a finger and a thumb near it, remaining to be seen for some while afterwards.

The Language of Computers

Edward J. Lias

In spite of the jokes and cartoons to the contrary, the general public has accepted with surprising ease the presence of a new medium which, more than radio or television, has the potential of revolutionizing life and human behavior.

Since computers were first used as mathematical problem solvers, people who had long ago made friends with the cash register in the grocery store felt that no real threat was impending, for the computer appeared to be an improved adding machine working faster and solving bigger problems. For gadgets which can calculate moon orbits, payrolls, and Easter dates to the year 4000 appear to be easily explainable as simple adding machines running extremely fast, and everyone knows that machines are benign idiots regardless of their speed.

The public image of computers rests on mechanical analogies and these images will be very slow to change so long as book clubs, credit cards, income-tax returns, and checking accounts are the only points of contact between people and computers, for these types of services blind us to the terrifying amperage which floats idling somewhere in printed circuitry. This power, if not measured before its release, may shock us by reshaping our culture and values.

In order to meter this power, the public must increasingly perceive that the computer is a medium, a vehicle for manipulating messages. The computer qualifies as a medium as much as any of the other media of communication surrounding us, and as such it can control our lives in unsuspected ways. If the reader has difficulty comparing computers to television or telephones, this is in part because very little has been written in the popular press about information retrieval (known as IR) and computer-aided instruction (CAI), the two roles in which computers far outdistance television as a language or medium by transmitting messages between men and relating people to people.

The significance of the computer as a message carrier is, as in most other media, ignored as though the computer were a neutral channel waiting to pass messages with no real biases of its own. The purpose of this essay is to help raise to conscious attention the special biases which the computer, as a medium, imposes on all people who modulate it with data.

The profound facility of computers to manipulate symbolic information—to instantly restructure and analyze data—causes me to assert that computers could potentially alter national and global culture by subliminally restructuring the metaphors on which present human perceptions build.

The breadth of this assertion seems bold only because old concepts lure us for the moment into believing that computers are simple amplifications of machines which we had before, similar to shifting a factory into a higher gear, or putting extra voltage into an adding machine to make it count faster. At present there seems to be no believable analogy by which to

In this remote skier's hut at the Winter Olympics, Grenoble, France, computing equipment can be seen. The games could not proceed without computers to schedule events, record and compare the speeds of runs, and dispense the records via multimedia information networks.

describe the difference of *magnitudes* when a word is held in the memory of a computer *not* by the angle of a mechanical gear, or by the turning of clumsy motors, but in pure electrical energy, *so that in this form every single word is instantly relatable to every other word in its memory.* This is a phenomenon which may not exist anywhere in nature except perhaps in a biological cell, where miraculous communication between thousands of individual parts appears to allow each part to relate directly to every other part. Perhaps some biological analogy for computers is what we need.

The ease of reorganizing information is usually demonstrated by such illustrations as this: eighty-six items of census statistics from sixty-nine countries are fed into a console. In three minutes the typewriter prints out complete population projections for the next 150 years, together with birth rates and growth rates and so forth, for *each* of the sixty-nine countries. Comparisons between countries and further statistics can be requested. With a desk calculator this might have been completed (inaccurately) in sixty-nine months.

This illustration, so typical of what the public reads, tends unfortunately to reinforce the old high-voltage adding-machine simile. To state that the Central Intelligence Agency stores 300,000 books in one desk-size space, or that a whole library can be carried in one hand with the entire Bible on a two-inch-square chip (National Cash Register Company) only projects the image of old technologies speeded up.

What easy explanation could project the following metamorphosis? A clacking, crawling adding machine enters an electronic cocoon to be given a memory for storing data, to be robbed of nearly all moving parts to make room for 100,000 transistors, and to be given the ability to alter its operating instructions *by itself* on the basis of stored data or evolving solutions. Obviously the resulting device bears no resemblance to its paleolithic ancestor. The new creation is at times able to achieve unpredictable, creative solutions via routes the programmer never thought of and never knows even when he checks out the final results. Some self-organizing "machines" (known as SOM) show a capacity to learn, observe, and remember relationships discovered in their own circuitry and never exposed to the user. In some experiments the results are verifiable but unexplainable; that is, the device could not by the programmed logic have found the resulting truth given the input data.

In order to probe the subliminal changes which computers will increasingly impose on the cultures which accept them, let us consider the computer in several of its media roles, functioning as a message bearer between peoples and places. And because computers are a silent language, being vehicles for thought transferral, we should search for the basic grammar of computers: their syntax, vocabulary, and subtle metaphors.

In the first place, we must recognize that *better than television, writing, speech, or any other medium, computers can instantly retrieve and sort information.*

Fantastic networks of computers which store books and essays are presently linked together around the United States via wires, microwave channels, and radio. Global connections between computers are nearly automatic with existing satellites. *Four hundred separate networks exist today.* Seven of these store more than 300,000 documents or abstracts (each).

Who Safeguards Privacy in This Medium?

As we go through life, we leave behind a trail of records. Today, these records are widely dispersed and generally inaccessible without a great deal of effort and diligence. The cost of such data collection is great, especially without an individual's cooperation. However, in the future this information will be centralized and easily accessible (at least to some people). Thus, a person will never be able to escape his past. Consequently, safeguards will have to be built into our information systems to provide the privacy required and due each individual in our society.

Computer Digest, March 1967

NASA has more than 600,000 abstracts stored in electronic memory with many terminals around the country at which scientists can reason with the computer, finally allowing it to select the ten or twenty documents which are most relevant to the researcher's interest. EDUCOM is in the process of linking 180 campuses together in twenty-nine states and Canada. The libraries of each school can effectively be available to all others. The State University of New York SUNY system links its fifty-nine schools similarly. M.I.T. is pursuing every conceivable angle of library data storage with its project INTREX, cooperating with many other schools. Harvard, Yale, and Columbia Universities have an information-retrieval system linking their three medical libraries, making more than 1,250,000 documents available to researchers at each of the schools and other points as well.

Without special training a user sits before a typewriter keyboard which has a small television screen above it. Every letter typed by the user appears on the screen and also registers in the computer memory at some other location. The user is guided by the computer to type highly specific requests, after which the computer scans its entire library to pick out those documents which satisfy the user (e.g., "I wish to see every document on heart transplants, but if related to fish or animals, or if written before 1966, don't send it. However, if Dr. Christiaan Barnard is mentioned let me see it. Otherwise also reject all authors except American and German. Inform me of movies and taped conferences available.") Instantly the researcher can begin scanning through abstracts and, later, pages of the material. If something on the screen is highly valuable, for a nominal fee he can have a photocopy of whatever was there.

What new warpage of perceptual foundations will occur when one is in weekly or daily friendship with such a symbol-manipulating medium?

Users of such equipment will probably begin to desire simultaneity in other areas of life and culture. Instantaneity. All-at-once-ness. The most-noticed quality of a computer regardless of its application is its blinding speed—or, better, *instancy.* Never before was there a way to cast an omniscient eye across every page of one million books ,so as to find (instantly) *every* place where a drug or legal trial is mentioned. One would be hard pressed to find every occurrence of the word "heart" in a 100-page book using visual search methods. (How many times has the letter *h* been used in this essay? How often was it used in words which also contained the letter *s*?) But in the language of computers the whole world of information is instantly sortable and available.

Already, selected scholars are permitted to type their new untested ideas directly into the system without having them first published in book form. Within hours a scholar in another country may detect those paragraphs and immediately rebuff the idea with several paragraphs of his own invention, after which third and fourth parties join the dialogue. But metaphors of simultaneity do not develop when there is a five-*year* delay requiring one to write a book, select a publisher, and have the book printed and distributed, whereupon someone else buys it, places it on a shelf for three years, then reads it, then says, "Bad idea."

Every room in the Rand Corporation building in Santa Monica, California, presently has outlet plugs for "computer power" as conveniently placed as electric outlets in homes. Information is not hard to come by. It is all instantly commandable. A Bell Telephone invention can pass every letter in a ten-thousand-volume library to another point *anywhere* in fifteen minutes. In which room will you install your information?

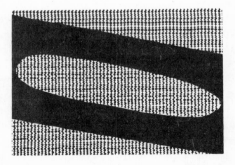

The eye of this small needle encircles more than 2000 bits of information which when played back may produce pictures, sounds, graphs, or sentences. Lawrence Radiation Laboratory stores a trillion bits of information in this way. Photo courtesy of IBM.

Computers Care If You
Don't Want Salt
in Your Airline Dinner!

Three large-scale Univac 1108-II systems, which will form the heart of what Univac describes as the world's largest commercial real-time electronic information network, have been installed at United Air Lines suburban Chicago computer center. Total cost of the "Unimatic" system will be $67 million. It is expected to be fully operational by this fall, linking 116 cities in United's 18,000-mile system by more than 100,000 miles of leased data links.

Electronic Data Processing Weekly, January 22, 1968

The shrinking size and cost of the equipment may eventually make it as popular as television. Paul Armer of the Rand Corporation seriously predicts that in ten years the souvenir when visiting a computer factory will be a tie clip containing a reject computer. At that size computers can be installed on the back of typewriters or in cars, with one for the family heritage of ideas, several in each classroom, and so on. IBM *presently* markets a baseball-size "memory" weighing two and a half pounds with one moving part and storage for 600,000 bits of data.

Human beings are able to make sense of the world because of their *simultaneous* coordination of six or seven sensory inputs (eyes, ears, and so on) within one central nervous system of experience. Man is an interacting place where all kinds of impressions exchange with each other and are recorded as a uniquely personal memory. What if the language of computers could enable *people* to similarly relate to each other in a national or global nerve? Perhaps then a global consciousness could develop as each person exchanges with and relates to all other people. Today dairymen, farmers, trucking firms, and so forth are called to small-town meetings where they are told of computer networks which apply to their endeavors. Farmers can dial into a computer network and get constantly updated information on fertilizers or the breeding of steers, *a practice which links them to the simultaneity of global markets* and makes possible instant feedback adjustment to world needs and values. Hail, global nervous systems!

In a culture which has already been primed to accept superimposed front and back views in nearly every telecast, permitting simultaneous sights to enter the eye the same as simultaneous sounds have always entered the ear, might not the creation of a supermedium which offers supersimultaneity be a hypnotic force for change in our culture? Hypnotic, that is, unless we broadcast its secrets and consciously focus upon them.

Some previews of how a culture may adapt its social customs to the language of computer-instancy can already be seen. One engineer wishes to encourage easy (fast, instant) interchange within the first two minutes of meeting a stranger. He proposes that everyone carry a card with holes punched in it indicating his interests and achievements. Thus, on meeting, the strangers could superimpose cards and interpret the spots through which light shines. If you presently enjoy the introductory scenes of ABC's *Wide World of Sports,* where four or five different sports are superimposed, then you may eventually want to treat people the same way. And without safeguards the computer will amplify this urge.

No wonder so many college students are willing to return computer questionnaires with a fee entitling them to a computer-matched date. It is so instant! And a chain of seventy-five gasoline stations is installing an automated means of buying emergency groceries while waiting for the gas tank to fill up. By the time the tank is full, an attendant hands his customer the packaged goods (choice of fifty items), which can be charged on the gasoline credit card.

Instead of lonely factory foremen barking, "Let's not waste any time around here," the whole culture may demand its goods and services to be *here now* (just like its information) *immediately.* We must ponder the eventual styling of social institutions after metaphors of instancy.

We should also recognize that *computers are a supermedium when they function as tutors in classrooms.*

RCA WILL DEMONSTRATE an electronic classroom system built around a Spectra 70 computer and TV displays at the HemisFair '68 International Exposition in San Antonio, Tex. this summer. Following the close of HemisFair in October, the system will be used by the Inter-American Education Center, San Antonio, as the nucleus of a state-wide computer complex for schools. It will aid in educating 180,000 pupils in the 14-county Texas School Region 20 and assist in handling the region's administrative functions.

*Electronic Data Processing
Weekly,* January 29, 1968

Thousands of students at all school levels are *today* being taught by computer-aided instruction (CAI), a trend which is sweeping the country. Far more than a pepped-up teaching machine, these consoles are able to monitor every fact retained by the student in an evolving process of learning. They automatically branch away from the subject to give special guidance when the student is uninformed on some point. The best-equipped school at this time (in this technique) is probably the University of California at Irvine, where, by 1980, 27,000 students will be instructed via such consoles.

The student presses a start button and the typewriter suggests, "INPUT YOUR NUMBER." The student types in "78K3319872." The computer types back, "OH, HELLO HELEN. IS WEDNESDAY SUCH A BAD DAY FOR STUDYING PHYSICS?" Then begins an interchange of fact presentation, question, answer, mistake, and so on. The computer judges each right or wrong response not in a linear judgment, but in relation to every other past response and every fact not yet presented, thus using a *process* evaluation. If the computer senses that the student is having a slow learning day (headache, perhaps) the computer is more patient and explanatory. If slowness of retention continues (sour love affair, perhaps), the computer will descend to a slower rate of presentation until it detects that comprehension is improving.

Dial-a-Paper System At Westinghouse Electric

The forerunner of a "dial-a-paper" system whereby the contents of thousands of books, magazines and newspapers can be made available via a telephone-television information retrieval system is being installed at the Westinghouse Electric Corporation's motor division in Buffalo, New York.

Engineers at the Westinghouse facility will be provided with touchtone telephones at their desks. To request a drawing, the engineer merely touchtones a number that connects him to the retrieval system. He then touch-tones the document number, type of document, his own telephone number, and his department code and employee number. In the case of active drawings, the request is filled in two seconds by the system and a copy made and sent to the engineer.

The system is so designed that in the future each engineer will have a video display unit on his desk. When he wants to see a document—and the system will store up to 10 million of them—he can have it displayed on the crt screen.

Similar systems can be produced for home use.

Data Processing Magazine,
December 1967

Photo courtesy of Sperry Rand Corp.

Clearly in the language of computers each student will subliminally notice that the entire syntax of the process places meaning and value in the retention of facts in the mind, after which the student may tend to judge other human beings the same way the computer has judged him. This neurotic fascination with fact retention is especially bizarre when the information systems previously described eliminate the need for interiorizing some given structure of facts; for the retrieval system could have structured it instantly in all possible ways. Could this throw us back to the "high standards" ages when information was hard to get and people could still control others by virtue of possessing a few more facts than their fellows?

Interviews with thirty students at Stanford University who were taking Russian from a computer revealed that all thought highly of their tutor. "The computer never embarrasses me; my other language instructor does." "It is infinitely patient with me." "It prints out a textbook just for me, spending extra time on my weak points. No one else has a textbook quite like mine." "It prints out weekend reviews when I request it."

What new warpage of perceptual foundations will occur when one is in daily contact with such a Socrates?

Students at these consoles will probably begin to respect the *process* adjustments which are made for each atom of learning. In fact the ability of the computer to monitor every single answer of the student and automatically to adjust the learning process makes the student the respected partner in a highly individual *process* which no human teacher (or mother) could ever bother to dignify with full attention.

A man riveting on an assembly line cannot get a picture of the whole process. Even executives rarely have an overview which takes into account *each* assembly-line rivet as a changing part of a changing whole. Yet, when computers monitor and direct assembly lines, each screw, wire, nut, color, and odor is measured against the total process, which is in a constant state of flux. Automatic feedback from every event in the process brings an end to metaphors based on linearity and straight-line sequences. For the first time, life and learning may be appreciated in terms of a fluctuating, ever-changing *process*. Students who respond poorly to written facts are automatically favored with graphics rather than lengthy typewritten presentations. No longer is there one set of linear lecture notes to which all students must mechanically respond or fail. It would even be possible to get to the Civil War before Thanksgiving.

The power-lawnmower generation may never understand the "process generation." The suburban masses enjoy the linearity of putting gasoline in one end and getting whirling blades out the other. By analogy a computer would constantly have to monitor the oil level, the clacking wrist pins, and everything, *readjusting all the other parts when any one factor changed* so as to maintain an unchanged whirling of the blade. A computer maintains an overview, caring about the process as opposed to the mere end result.

Dr. Suppes at Stanford University has about 1200 children (grades one through six) learning all subjects (spelling, fractions, history, and so forth) from such consoles. These children will never be unfamiliar with computer noises, sights, benefits, *processes*. What foundational structures of mind will they grow up to have? How will the grouping of their senses be altered? Will they interpret the ear in metaphors of the eye? Or the eye in metaphors of the ear? Will they structure their social habits after the media which surround them?

In the third place, we must recognize that *computers, being a powerful medium, will affect the other message systems in the culture—especially the English language.*

Hundreds of thousands of people (some of them in grade school) are being prepared to cope with a new and distinct language or set of communicative habits. The language of computers is part math, part mystery. Part letters, part numbers. Part logic, part English. Attempts to explain computers at parties generally fail.

At the present time, the general public knows very little about computers. The computer vocabulary is so limited for the public that easy verbalizing cannot occur. Words such as "programming," "punchcard," "spindle," "mutilate," "IBM" and a few others form the ill-defined image of an unknown god to whom the masses pay a grudging homage.

Not that technical jargon is underdeveloped. The people who work with the equipment can join the club only after learning to handle fluently the 8500 technical words listed in Charles J. Sippl's *Computer Dictionary and Handbook.* "Isochronous modulation," "FORTRAN," "invariant imbedding," "interface," "buffer," and so on give the technician the power to style his equipment to his purpose. According to projections given in the 1967 edition of *Moody's Computer Industry Survey,* by 1971 at least 75,000 computers will be in use in the United States alone. Scouts are searching for 350,000 people who do not now work in this field to be trained within the next three years so that the industry may go on, which means that a lot of people are going to be telling about or hearing about computers. The chances of computer metaphors, syntax, and vocabulary *not* affecting the English language are very slim.

Inasmuch as the English language is constantly changing, one might wonder why the further changes which computers may impart to it are worthy of attention or conscious appraisal. The monumental significance of changes in language are asserted because of the following propositions.

1. The structure and lexicon of our language governs our perception of the world around us. To change language is to change one's operational world.

2. Our level of consciousness is directly related to the hierarchical labeling "tricks" of language. Idea formulation is not independent of language. (Try to mentally rearrange the things in your room for which there are no words.)

3. To add metaphors, words, styles, etc. to a language is to raise (or perhaps change) the degree of consciousness of the peoples who habitually use that language.

4. We cannot speak coherently without adhering *absolutely* to the organization and classifications of the language. The power to alter these patterns cannot be regarded as superficial.

The number of touchpoints between computers and language are so numerous as to *force* speedy changes in written/ spoken English and styles of expression. The list below preludes the inter-electro-lingua mergence.

1. Russian and German scientific abstracts are being translated into English via computers. This linguistic stunt limits vocabulary and, so far, encourages to some extent a mechanistic style of essay.

2. Nearly all computers *type out* replies to various inputs, usually in upper-case letters exclusively.

3. Some computers now respond to *spoken* commands, requiring new etiquette and keeping of rules of outspoken office managers.

4. Some can scan pages, "reading" letters and numbers directly from the page into their memory, forcing a limit on the style of alphabet which may be used, the shape of each letter being dictated by the electronic eye.

5. Some can actually generate and "speak" English words, thus talking to people in the room. This is not the playing of a pre-recorded tape. Rather, the computer generates each phoneme and syllable, planning the spacing so as to form words and sentences. The Voice Answer Back (VAB) system used on the New York Stock Exchange is widely versatile in this facility.

6. Books, essays, and pictures can be stored in computer memory for later retrieval or specific ideas in those texts. The number of times that "assassination" appears in sentences which also contain the word "conspiracy" can be queried and accurately determined as the computer scans its entire memory of books and pages in a few seconds.

7. With the new laser memories which are now working experimentally, computers could potentially store *every* word written globally every day if there should be reason and motive for doing so. Regardless, English will be mingled with other languages increasingly via the retrieval networks as they span continents and oceans.

8. According to a recent survey, by 1975 nearly all of our 25,000 high schools will require courses in data processing

before graduation. New words and imagery will be known to everyone thereafter.

9. More than 260 computer publications and journals help to spread the electronic lexicon all around.

10. Special computer languages exist for the people who program the equipment. "COBAL," "PL/1," "FORTRAN," and others are interlanguages between people and computers, enabling the circuitry to regard everything as on-off, yes-no experiences.

11. The country which first develops global information networks will spread its language with phenomenal abandon. Present United States satellites together with President Johnson's request for central data banks indicate that English may soon be accepted as the official language for information.

12. The experimental insertion of microcircuits into dogs' brains, transmitting information directly into the brain apart from the senses, may indicate that language could eventually be bypassed as the most common human information input. With plug-in jacks on the side of our heads, gruesome opportunities for control of thought and behavior would arise.

13. Since computers are limited in memory size, users do not load unnecessary adjectives, synonyms, phrases, letters, or punctuation into the memory. Hence, with reductions of synonyms, the English lexicon may become more technical (less abstract, more special), with fewer mutiple meanings. The abbreviated spellings point in the direction of a monosyllabic vocabulary.

If the telegraph, telephone, LP records, radio, and television have changed our language, how much more will computers change it?

The computer will work a hideous subversion on society if we talk much longer about this instantaneous symbol handler with mechanical, time-oriented words. To speak of computers in parables which hide their processing innards will make us prey to their sullen tyranny. The troublesome, blinding, comforting comparison is MACHINE! Do not think of computers as machines. They are speed-of-light-blenders-of-fragments-into-unforeseen-unities.

The best thing that could happen would be for the children

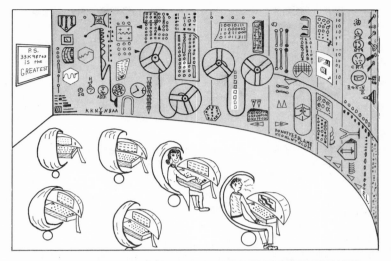

"PUSH THE HARMONIC PHASEOVER DELINEATORS BEFORE YOU
SEQUENCE THE MODULE INTERFACE DETECTORS, stupid!"

now sitting at consoles to adopt a "bathroom" or "kitchen" metaphor in which, just as certain things are done in a special place called "kitchen," after which the kitchen is left for the other interests of life, so also one takes care of his information needs in a "computer room," after which he goes out to be a social being. Power-lawnmower metaphors have conned us into organizing other human beings as though they, too, should be mechanical, linear, and predictable. Let us hope the nonlinear computer *processes* will help us to break that unfortunate and inadequate way of talking and thinking about life.

Perhaps the coming generation who were computer-tutored will not be handicapped by our outdated fascination with mechanics. When we lived near machines, we were driven, via mechanical metaphors and analogies, to make all the rest of life like machines. And then we felt loss of identity. But the coming generation may not be in an identity crisis with machines. Being one of the mechanical dolls, this author cannot help feeling a loss of identity when his name becomes a set of numbers rather than the equally arbitrary set of letters. Is not 33K82957 a euphoneous, uniquely beautiful, individual identification label? But the "instant generation" may feel no need to demonstrate against the removal of letters from telephone numbers. Having befriended the supermedium from childhood, they will feel no ego threat. Their acceptance of speed-of-light/process metaphors may be the new language in America: a new set of symbols permitting a new view of man, one in which he accepts as pleasure the amplification of his mind. And the new language has the potential to foster the peaceful evolution of a global brain cell.

UCC Sets Up Global Computer Network

University Computing Co., a Dallas-based computer services company, has set up a multinational computer utility network.

The four-and-a-half-year-old concern is projecting an investment of more than $100 million in the next three years in developing this international web. About $25 million is already invested.

The projection includes major centers in the U.S. and in foreign countries plus hundreds of satellite operations tied into each of the major centers.

Under the utility concept, UCC supplies computer problem-solving capabilities to geographically dispersed users.

At present, the company has overseas computer services capabilities in Birmingham and London, England; Shannon, Ireland, and technical assistance groups in Melbourne, Australia, and Caracas, Venezuela.

UCC currently has computer utility centers in the U.S. in Los Angeles, Tulsa, Houston, Dallas and New York City.

Business Automation,
January 1968

Senator Long Says
Inefficiency Is Privacy Guard!

WASHINGTON, D.C.— "Whatever privacy remains for the American citizen . . . remains because the Federal Government is presently too inefficient to pull all its personal information files together." This statement by Senator Edward Long, chairman of the Subcommittee on Administrative Practice and Procedure, is one of the most dramatic and recent comments on a proposed data bank for the government.

Long also said, in a 605 page summary, that the data bank would make it very easy to "put a whole life history no further than the push of a button away."

Experts Testify

The subcommittee has heard testimony by Alan Westin (School of Government,

Columbia) suggesting that citizens be given property rights to their own data.

Wiley Branton (United Planning Organization) felt that personal data on the nation's poor—particularly those eligible under one of the government's poverty programs—should be protected by a three-man regulatory agency. Branton also asked that the FBI explain what protection is given for individual privacy under the crime data system now in operation.

Cashless-Checkless Society

Long also pointed to another serious privacy threat—completely computerized banking, leaving us a "cashless-checkless society."

Computerworld,
February 21, 1968

Some Questions Which Remain

1. Does the world *need* more efficient handling of information? Does an instantaneous handling of letters and numbers bear any correlation to the problems of overpopulation, mass starvation, or air pollution?

2. Will a critical point ever be reached when people will seek refuge *from* information rather than welcoming all media into their bedrooms?

3. If the extension of man's muscles in the form of machines guaranteed the building of social institutions after mechanical models, may not the extension of man's nerves in the form of computer networks stimulate the rebuilding of govern-

ments, schools, bureaucracies, and architecture after electronic metaphors?

4. Do you feel as though a child is sticking out his tongue at you when a machine hands you a toll ticket? If it were a human slave, would you feel better? Why do we want people to do what machines can do?

5. If the printing press encouraged people to treat other people like moveable type, eventually placing machines and bureaucracies between people (rather than speech and touch), will the electronic processing of our writings, machines, and bureaucracies encourage more distance or less distance between people? Nations?

6. Should we ponder number five further?

7. Did the word *computer* occur exactly 236 times in this essay?

8. Does the fact that people are against computers when they have never used them, neutral when near them, and transfixed when operating them indicate a widespread human hypnosis under which gadgetry can alter beliefs more certainly than books, churches, lectures, schools, and blood relatives?

9. Or do all media possess this power?

The Language of the Cold War

Jerome D. Frank

The nuclear arms race poses a mortal and increasingly pressing danger to civilization. It is obvious that the chief source
of peril lies not in the nuclear weapons but in the human
beings behind them, and that therefore the danger can only
be resolved by changes in human attitudes. As a psychiatrist
I have been struck by certain parallels between the behavior
of nations today and that of mental patients. Though such
parallels are always open to question, calling attention to
them may serve to stimulate thinking about the human
problems of the arms race.

The prize for which the United States and Russia are
unwittingly contending is mutual destruction, yet neither side
seems able to change its course of action. A nuclear accident
or error of judgment which could trigger a full-scale war
becomes more probable with each passing day, as the power
to fire nuclear weapons becomes ever more widely diffused and
the warning time for effective retaliation steadily decreases.
A year ago General Omar Bradley put it this way: "We are
now speeding inexorably toward a day when even the inge-
nuity of our scientists may be unable to save us from the
consequences of a single rash act or a lone reckless hand upon
the switch of an uninterceptorable missile."

Society reacts to this terrifying situation in two characteristic ways, both of which impede its solution. One is a remarkable indifference, probably best illustrated by the almost total
apathy concerning civil defense in both Russia and the United
States; the other is the building of still more nuclear weapons,
thereby intensifying the behavior which created the problem
in the first place. Psychiatrists are familiar with both types
of reaction in their patients and have termed them "denial"
and "repetition compulsion."

In psychiatric jargon, denial is a patient's attempt to deal
with a massive threat by denying its existence. Examples are
the patient with blindness due to brain disease who insists

173

that he can see, or the patient in the back ward of a mental hospital who maintains that she is in a palace. The term is also used, perhaps unwarrantably, for the refusal of some mortally ill patients to accept the imminence of death. Since death is inevitable, it is perhaps just as well that no human being can steadily contemplate his own demise. In fact, without this safety device, life would probably be unbearable. So it is understandable that each person sees himself as surviving a nuclear war, and this is not affected by the fact that millions are faced with death simultaneously.

It is particularly easy to deny the dangers of nuclear weapons because they are both unprecedented and impalpable. Nuclear energy is of an order of magnitude far beyond anything human beings have experienced before, except possibly those who live on the slopes of volcanoes. The vast majority of Americans have never experienced even the destruction wrought by conventional weapons. Our land has not directly suffered war for about one hundred years, and then only a small area was involved. It is impossible to imagine the destructive power of twenty million tons of TNT, which a single hydrogen bomb can generate, much less what it would mean if hundreds or thousands of hydrogen bombs exploded. Moreover, the nuclear threat does not impinge on any of the senses. Submarines lurking offshore, airplanes miles overhead, poised guided missiles thousands of miles away, even strontium 90 nibbling at our bone marrow are all tasteless, odorless, silent, invisible, and impaipable. As a result it requires a constant effort of imagination to be aware of their presence.

Denial of a danger prevents taking action to remove it. If the problem does not exist psychologically, there is no incentive to do anything about it. When death is threatened from sources beyond human control, denial is as good a way of handling it as any, since nothing can be done. But when the death threat is of human making and can be removed by human beings, then the tendency to deny its existence is tragic.

More alarming than the tendency to deny the dangers of the nuclear arms race is the fact that attempts to find solutions lead only to intensification of a course of action which enhances the danger. Why can we not change behavior which we know is only making matters worse? One reason may be that we are frightened, and anxiety if too strong tends to make rigid both perception and behavior.

Patients with emotional illness often show remarkable rigidity of behavior, which Freud labeled the repetition compulsion. They keep repeating the very acts which cause trouble for them. This seems to be partly a result of their chronic anxiety. The patient clings to a faulty solution to a problem because he is afraid to give it up. The more anxious a person is, the more rigid his behavior tends to become. Similarly, the more menacing the arms race becomes, the more frantically we build more weapons and the less we seem able to seek more sensible alternatives. Anxiety also tends to freeze one's perceptions of the world. There is nothing harder to stand than ambiguity, so when faced with a dangerous situation one tends to oversimplify it. Everything becomes black and white. To use a technical term, thinking tends to become stereotyped.

This is seen clearly in the stereotype of "the enemy." No matter who the enemy is or who we are, the enemy tends to be perceived as intellectually inferior but possessed of an animal cunning which enables him easily to outwit us. The enemy is seen as cruel, treacherous, and bent on aggression. Our side is seen as intellectually superior but guileless and therefore easily victimized, peace-loving, honorable, and fighting only in self-defense. These stereotypes are probably as old as the human race and may be related to the fact that we are group animals. All gregarious creatures from ants to man automatically fear and hate the stranger, and whenever a group feels threatened by another, these primeval feelings reassert themselves. It is remarkable how rapidly the stereotype of the enemy can be shifted from one group to another. Scarcely more than a decade ago, Germany and Japan were cast in this role and Russia was our noble ally. Russia has now changed places with Germany and Japan, and we are not even embarrassed by the memory of our recent pictures of these three countries.

The fact that the enemy—whoever he may be—is viewed as completely untrustworthy is a major source of tensions leading to war.

The terrible thing about the mutual distrust of enemies is that it is justified. Some enemies are untrustworthy to begin with, but all become so eventually. Enemies cannot trust each other because each is forced to act in such a way as to justify the other's misgivings. This is an example of what the sociologist Robert K. Merton has termed the "self-fulfilling prophecy."

The operation of the self-fulfilling prophecy is perhaps best seen in the behavior of individuals. All social behavior tends to elicit corresponding behavior from the person toward whom it is directed. Friendliness begets a friendly response, hostility a hostile one. So if you expect someone to react to you in a certain way, you may act toward him in such a manner that he reacts in the way you predicted. Thus you cause your own prophecy to be fulfilled.

This can be seen most clearly in psychiatric patients, because of the rigidity of their behavior. A good example is the paranoid patient who expects everyone to be his enemy. You may be disposed to be friendly when you first meet him. Since he is sure you hate him, however, he persistently rebuffs your advances and maintains a surly, suspicious manner. In the face of this you are very apt to come to dislike him. Thus he succeeds in confirming his prophecy that everyone is against him, and will be even more suspicious of the next person he meets.

The same kind of mechanism operates at the level of societies. Russia and the United States each claim to base their foreign policy on the premise that the other would attack if it dared, and so each behaves in such a way as to make an attack increasingly likely. As General Douglas MacArthur pointed out in a speech to the American Legion in 1955, present tensions are "kept alive by two great illusions. The one, a complete belief on the part of the Soviet world that the capitalist powers are preparing to attack it; that sooner or later we intend to strike. And the other, a complete belief on the part of the capitalist countries that the Soviets are preparing to attack us. Both are wrong. Each side, so far as the masses are concerned, is equally desirous of peace. For either side, war with the other would mean nothing but disaster. Both equally dread it. But the constant acceleration of preparation may well, without specific intent, ultimately produce a spontaneous combustion."

The mutual expectancy of Russia and the United States that the other plans to attack leads each to negotiate to gain a supposed advantage, intensifying the mutual distrust. Russia wanted to ban atomic weapons when we alone had them; we want to ban outer space as an area of conflict now that Russia seems to be ahead in this field. We ring Russia with bomber and missile bases, she treacherously crushes Hungary and develops ICBM's, each thereby strengthening the other's fear of attack and increasing the probability that it will occur.

Another source of our inability to break out of our suicidal behavior pattern is that the existence of limitless destructive energy has drastically changed the traditional meanings of certain words and phrases, such as "defense," "national security," and "balance of power." Use of these in their former meanings has become so automatic that we no longer subject them to critical scrutiny, especially since their connotations are reassuring. As a result, we may commit ourselves to a false conclusion even before we have started to think. It is especially hard to realize that the words are being misused because everyone does it from partisans of world government to isolationists. Moreover the misuse is casual, as if it were self-evident, which helps it to escape critical scrutiny.

For example, we automatically refer to our nuclear arms policy as one of defense, yet there is no defense against nuclear weapons in the strict sense of the term. According to the dictionary, "defense" is "the state of being defended," and "defend" is defined as "to shield from attack or violence, protect." In pre-atomic days it was a comforting thought that for each new offense weapon, a genuine defense was eventually developed. Even though the protection it afforded was never perfect, it was adequate. Today, when one fighter-bomber with nuclear weapons carries more destructive power than all the bombers in World War II, a defense that is even 90 per cent effective would not prevent vast destruction. What is really meant by defense today is deterrence through threat of retaliation. But in using the word "defense" to justify continued arming, we automatically slip into thinking of it in its old connotation. For example, Robert Nathan recently spoke of our creating a "massive defensive shield." There is no shield against nuclear weapons, but only a precarious "balance of terror" which is, at best, a brief reprieve and which may, with luck, gain us enough time to find a better solution.

Another phrase which no longer means anything is "balance of power," and concepts implied by it, such as "catching up" with the Russians, are equally meaningless. For phrases implying relative strength have no meaning when each side can destroy the other many times over. What does "catch up" mean when, according to President Eisenhower, we can already bring "near annihilation" to Russia? And how do we know when we have caught up? We are said to have about 35,000 atom bombs; Russia, 10,000. Are we balanced or not?

A third phrase which is rapidly losing its meaning is "national security." These words imply that one nation can be secure at the expense of the security of other nations. No nation can control the fall-out it receives from atomic explosions anywhere in the world; soon no nation will be able to control its own weather. Every inch of the globe can soon come under observation or attack from earth satellites. Those who think in terms of national security already foresee America fighting Russia for control of the moon. In today's world, either all nations are secure or none is.

Finally, there is the word "stalemate." Those who feel we must continue the arms race argue that if we maintain the stalemate long enough, eventually things will somehow work out. This term, derived from chess, conjures up an image of static deadlock which involves no further threat to either side. The arms race is far from static. Each day it continues increases the chances of mutual destruction and decreases the chances of peaceful accommodation. The use of "stalemate" to describe this state of affairs can only lead to faulty thinking and a false sense of security.

One sign that a person's thinking processes have gone seriously awry is inability to detect absurdities. For example, if a patient can see nothing wrong with the statement, "Bill Jones's feet are so big he has to put his pants on over his head," psychiatrists worry about the intactness of his intellectual processes. Our failure to take account of the changed meanings of words leads us to make statements which are almost as absurd. A recent editorial in the Baltimore *Sun* spoke of "the grim business of balancing power against power as our only means of assuring peace." How can balancing power against power, which in the past has led only to war, assure peace? And what does it mean to balance power against power after each side has enough power to destroy the other many times over? Pronouncements about American missile and bomber bases in the NATO countries contain a more striking absurdity, which passes unnoticed, perhaps because the contradictory thoughts do not occur in the same statement. The contradictory statements are that these bases will enable us to retaliate instantly, and that the missiles cannot be fired except after consulting with our allies.

This is the kind of semantic tangle in which we find ourselves today. We seem to have slipped into George Orwell's world of doublethink without knowing it.

To summarize: the inability of Russia and America to break out of the arms race may involve several psychological factors. Fear tends to make us deny the existence of the danger, especially since the threat lies outside previous experience. When we do face up to it, the same fear makes it difficult for each country to change the behavior which creates the danger, especially since each is forced to behave in such a way as to confirm the other's suspicions—the self-fulfilling prophecy.

These social attitudes are probably as old as mankind. In the past they have regularly led to wars which destroyed small portions of humanity. From the standpoint of the human race this was tolerable, for there were always enough survivors. Now, for the first time, these attitudes must be drastically modified if the human adventure is to continue. The task is made more difficult because nuclear energy has changed the traditional meanings of certain words that we habitually use in thinking about the issues of war and peace.

Psychotherapy tries to produce beneficial changes of attitude in individuals. Whether principles of psychotherapy can be applied to societies is highly questionable, but the implications of certain of these principles for halting the nuclear arms race may warrant exploration.

Psychotherapy tries to help the patient to see his problems and his faulty solutions more clearly, as the first step toward finding better ones. At the same time, by offering emotional support, the psychotherapist tries to reduce the patient's anxiety and help him to find the courage to experiment with more flexible, less stereotyped ways of perceiving others and behaving toward them. By improving his ability to communicate with others, the patient gains more satisfactions and suffers less frustrations, thereby diminishing his anxiety. Thus a process of progressive improvement may be started. For this process to succeed, the patient must have confidence that the therapist is competent to help him and has his welfare at heart.

In attempting to apply psychotherapeutic principles to today's sick world, the obvious question is: Who is to be the psychotherapist? Who has the confidence of both the United States and Russia, and is viewed by them as competent to resolve their differences? At first glance the question seems absurd, yet certain groups may potentially function in this way. The industrially backward and relatively unarmed nations, small and large, who can only lose by a nuclear war may be able through the United Nations gradually to modify the behavior of the major powers. Many nuclear physicists seem able to focus on the welfare of humanity regardless of the side of the Iron Curtain from which they come, and their prestige is great in all nations. That both Russia and the United States agreed to a conference to devise adequate measures of inspection of a test ban on nuclear weapons is a sign that both, at least provisionally, trust the other's scientists as well as their own.

Even in the absence of a psychotherapist, psychotherapeutic principles may be applicable to aspects of our present dilemma. For example, they suggest that it is vitally important for each person to make a constant effort to keep his thinking straight. One must fight the tendency to deny the extent and immediacy of the danger, and make sure the words one habitually uses in thinking about the problem are appropriate. Only in these ways can the real nature of the issues be kept clearly in mind.

The psychotherapeutic emphasis on improved communication seems especially relevant. Communication between Russians and Americans at every level should be encouraged. As we come to see each other engaged in our occupations at home, we may find grounds for mutual understanding which are now hidden by the stereotype of the enemy. Today Russian and American scientists collaborate successfully in the International Geophysical Year, athletes compete without bloodshed, and artists from each country have been enthusiastically welcomed in the other. So we may hope that expanded communication between Russia and the United States may, in time, help weaken the will of each to destroy the other without diminishing the will to compete by peaceful means.

But the beneficial effects of improved communication appear only slowly, and the danger increases rapidly. What is needed is a change in our behavior toward Russia today, especially at the conference table. We now enter into negotiations to call Russia's bluff or to justify further arming by proving that negotiations are futile. This guarantees failure and an intensification of mutual distrust. To break this vicious circle we would have to negotiate on the assumption that the Russians want peace as strongly as we do. Just as changing habitual neurotic behavior involves risk for a patient, so this change of attitude would also involve some risk, but it is not as great as the danger entailed by our present course. If we can look beyond our fears, there are signs that the risk may not be as great as we think. It is true that no country, including Russia and the United States, can be trusted when its vital interests are involved, but Russia has a vital interest in maintaining peace.

There is no doubt that Russia is bending every effort to make the entire world a Union of Soviet Socialist Republics, but she is achieving her goal so successfully by means short of war that she would seem to have much more to lose than to gain by trying to destroy us at great cost to herself. She knows much more of the horrors of war than we do. In the last war she lost an estimated 7 million soldiers and 20 million to 40 million civilians; we lost 300,000 soldiers and a negligible number of civilians. She is making immense strides in education, science, and industry; and despite our talking of catching up, her rate of gain in these areas far exceeds ours. She is being equally successful in winning the uncommitted nations by exporting technicians and doctors, increasing monetary aid, and, above all, by the example of a nation that has pulled itself up from an industrially backward country to a pre-eminent position in one generation.

Nor must it be assumed that the Russian and American ways of life will always be totally incompatible. Russia is still a ruthless dictatorship, but stirrings of freedom are discernible. Dr. Horsley Gantt, an American psychiatrist who speaks Russian fluently, was constantly accompanied by an interpreter on a visit to Russia some twenty years ago. On a recent trip he was allowed to go alone to visit his colleagues, and they were not afraid to receive him. News dispatches in the past year have contained many suggestions that political, industrial, legal, and agricultural policies are in flux, and transfer of power within Russia has become more peaceful and orderly. Although the treacherous execution of Nagy shows that Russia's policy toward the satellites is still one of terror, it may be significant that since the execution of Beria, no defeated Russian leader has been publicly killed.

If we and Russia can break away from the stereotype of each other as the enemy, we may be able to reach an agreement to stop testing nuclear weapons, with an arrangement for mutual inspection. Regardless of its effect on nuclear armaments, such an agreement, if it worked, would be of the utmost psychological importance. For it would be the first, and therefore the most crucial, step toward the establishment of mutual confidence. Then it would become possible to move further along the road to the ultimate goal: a general system for maintaining world peace and disarmament.

Poker, Pawns, and Power

Edward L. Katzenbach, Jr.[1]

The bar sinister on our national escutcheon is that we are and have been a nation of poker players.

Now, no doubt poker has its place. But I believe that the game has played deuces wild with our history and that it may, in fact, have as potentially a disastrous effect on the last half of the twentieth century as strip poker has on a college weekend.

Consider for one moment the damage that poker playing has had on the character of the nation. Note on your television set that at the moment of our greatest national glory, when the good guys are shooting up the bad guys in the West, the saloons in which the bad guys play poker have false fronts —ones which make buildings look as though they were two stories high when in fact they are only one. Besides, this nation originated the "false front" in men's shirtwear, and admitted the "front man" into the ranks of respectable wage earners. Why was the false front respectable throughout our history? Why is front itself so important? The answer, of course, is poker. For the essence of the game is front and bluff, with some odds thrown in. For those of us for whom candor is high in our system of values, and mathematics is low in the list of our abilities, the game is little better than banditry.

Besides, it is very dangerous in strategic terms.

Let me cite three reasons. In the first place, poker tends to make one think in terms of odds. But when one thinks in strategic terms, odds are hardly appropriate. For example, how would one respond to policy considerations which were couched in these terms: It's 3 to 1 that A and B will have a falling out, or 4 to 1 that the C will have the atomic bomb in three years, or 50 to 1 against the Canadians attacking the

[1] Former Deputy Assistant Secretary of Defense for Education and Manpower Resources.

Mexicans or vice versa? In the real world, what does one do with odds? The odds are that one rejects them.

Secondly, poker is not a game in which one can exercise flexibility. Indeed, it was the crass poker player who invented that phrase which we hear everywhere and all the time: "Put up or shut up." It does not seem to me, in a world in which the spectrum of threat is as wide as it is in ours, that one can expect any Chief Executive to say blatantly, "I'll call you on that one." This does not mean that I am not fully aware that there is a time to "put up or shut up" and to say candidly, "I call your bluff." But it does strike me that a game in which one raises the antes or surrenders one's hand is hardly applicable to the complex world in which we live.

Finally, poker leads to circuitous thinking. It starts with an *if,* ends with a *then,* and between them alternates pronouns before the verb *think.* It goes like this: "If he thinks that I think that he thinks that I think that he thinks, then. . . ." This type of thinking reminds me of the dodo bird, which thought flying in ever smaller concentric circles was fun—until it mysteriously disappeared.

Chess, on the other hand, is a different matter. A Jack of Hearts has no personality, but a Bishop does have. A King of Spades is no more a king than I am, but a King on a chessboard is a personage—one who moves slowly and deliberately in one direction or another, seldom making mistakes—but with, to be sure, no great vigor. His Queen, however, is obviously a Prime Minister. Her relationship to him is one frequently encountered wherever the chief of state is a figurehead and the Prime Minister, or whatever he may be called, does whatever is done.

It requires very little perception to see the relevance of chess to the strategic problems of our time—to raising standards of living, to guerrilla actions, and to the resolution of the Cold War. Notice that each of the pieces has characteristics of its own, and that each gains or loses in strength depending upon the confidence the player has in the piece and the positions of allied pieces. Can you think of anything more meaningful than this to a world in which the great power groupings have so much to gain by winning the confidence and building the prosperity of other nations? And finally, the chess player understands, as we all must understand, that there may be tactical advantages to retreats in seeking victory. He understands the most important factor of all—that a Pawn is not something to be taken lightly, for the least of the powers can not only get in the way but can actually bring about the downfall of figures more powerful.

If, then, the playing of chess is a habit to be cultivated so that men's minds can understand the problems of their day, and if it is true that the playing of poker instills habits of thought which are positively dangerous for the national well-being, it might be well, in the interest of national welfare, that the latter be banned and the former taught in each first grade in the nation.

The Voices of the Magazines

David Cort

First, one must stop looking for a single master tide running through American magazines. Everywhere opposite tides run against each other, setting up whirlpools, rips, and undertows. The Time Inc. style, considered revolutionary and (though not by me) vulgar, subverted the periodicals of the twenties and thirties, and compelled nearly everybody to imitate it. Its simple aim was to say anything as quickly and factually as possible. Thus (June 12, 1933): "Vexed last week was upright Winthrop Williams Aldrich, brother-in-law of John D. Rockefeller, Jr. and president of Chase Manhattan Bank (world's largest). And with good cause."

One cannot quite say that this style has swept journalism, but a listless imitation of it certainly has. Factualism now uses such pitiful cover formulae as "Surveys show . . ." to introduce an undocumented point, which is then further simplified on the cover to sell copies. Highly simplified points, based on *Time*'s "curt, clear, complete," are regularly made by the *Reader's Digest, Pageant, Coronet,* et al., and more urbanely by *Look* and *The Saturday Evening Post.* It should be noted that early *Time* style was a holy canon, devoutly ritualized; these others are merely bowing to a general consensus. The old muscle has gone; the fanatic factualism has become a crutch.

But an absolutely opposite style rolled on, as if *Time* had never been invented. The nonformula seductions of *Vanity Fair* vanished. But such magazines as *Vogue* and *Harper's Bazaar* were not swayed by a hair's breadth. Hysterical, allusive, metaphorical, their style was obliged to ascend to high C in four or five words, and so it continued to do, with the aid of a succession of *manquée* Mary McCarthys on the staff. While apparently a mere heresy for a time, this style conspicuously failed to shrink; instead, it *floriated.*

Taking a recent (November 1, 1967) *Vogue* at random: "The crash of velvet, . . . it's cymbolic . . ."; "Black velvet at its

187

most fatale . . ."; ". . . falls like a liquid-gold love note against the calf"; ". . . sumptuous and innocent like the young Edward in a Holbein portrait"; "great glossy, luxurious fluff of fur"; "actor with a sonar feeling for the meanings under words." Sometimes this language almost means something expressible. What rot is this about meanings under words? But yes, under *Vogue*'s words is the unstated, and unstatable, meaning that any female reader can escape from the miserable fact of herself into something cymbalic, fatale, sumptuous, glossy, luxurious, etc., etc., and into still other adjectives in the next issue of *Vogue* or *Harper's Bazaar,* and they have the young ladies to invent them. Still, this style makes a point: buy the stuff and you'll be cymbalic, etc. The magazine did not invent the idea that the lady could be more gorgeous or ravishing than she in fact is. The lady invented it. The magazine is only accommodating this conviction insofar as it can.

These two tides of Time Inc. and *Vogue–Harper's Bazaar,* while utterly ignoring one another (I have worked for all three organizations), seem to have met in a maelstrom in which the current journalist tries to swim. The style of Ian Fleming, Tom Wolfe, Jim Breslin, et al., is half-Time Inc. in its glut of factual details such as materials, brands, gun calibers, horsepowers, tailors, resorts, street addresses, etc. But the facts become insignificant, that is, are "thrown away" in a gush of psychedelic prose. Something real, but very large and undefined, is happening.

This style makes a simple point: you are hopelessly outside it all, unless, perhaps, you buy the designated motorcycle, clothing, tattoos, and learn how to kill people with your bare hands. A style that excludes the reader would turn repellent very quickly, if it did not offer paradise, and so it must do. For the moment, high fashion has conquered reality, *Vogue* has given *Time*-Sampson a haircut.

For here we find that *Vogue* style has infiltrated Time Inc. Again at random, *Life* (August 12, 1957) says: "The music . . . can sound like a cascade of spilled golden nails" or "Her incredible 6-foot-4 frame, collapsible like a spider and extensible to a sexy derrick. . . ."

How can one authenticate statements of this sort? I do not know how golden nails sound, when spilled, but I am certain it is not musical at all. A *Time* checker in the old days would have been fired, an hour after the writer had slunk into the night. And can spiders be described as collapsible or derricks as sexy? The answer is no. One *Life* picture story was actually "captioned" with Hindu poetry.

There has been a shocking failure of nerve on one side, none on the other. The old Time Inc. was trying to say that matters are exactly as they are, no more, no less, sometimes perhaps in areas where matters were not that simple. The effort, in my opinion, was worthy, if not always successful, and it was sincere. It might still be worthy today, but it would not be chic. The new shorn Time Inc. wants to get into the party, but not to bring down the temple.

Both sides constantly express the overpowering, the conquering cliché of the period: what's really happening? A decade or so ago, the question referred to Negroes; now it applies to children, who have appropriated the Negro style. The idea that children know something special (as if no adult had ever been a child) is now the terrified obsession of some editors. Their primary question is: what are these flocks of chickadees up to now? In fact, I have never heard of current juvenile lunacy that was not antedated by my friends and myself some forty years ago, except that we had some instinct for survival and self-respect. But all magazines like to present these misbehaviors as if they were fresh and thrilling, though horrifying, enormities. These editors, I suspect, are saying that they were never children.

Magazines have to report on the various enemies within the gates: the Mafia, the Unreconstructed South, "now" Youth, and also the angry Negroes, ignoring intelligent Italians, white Southerners, young people, and Negroes, because the enemy is exciting, the decent people are not.

The basic cliché of editorial writing, whether about Vietnam, poverty, Negroes, ghettos, crime, universal education, automation, parochial and private schools, or police procedures, is that each subject must be considered by itself in a vacuum. Yet all the subjects listed above are closely related. The political metaphor of Right, Left, Middle-of-the-Road inevitably reduces nearly every magazine's politics to a cliché. Surely there are other orders, such as realistic and idealistic, or magnanimous and selfish, or legalistic and humane. A pro-labor position is stamped liberal or Left, but for a union man it is not liberal or magnanimous or sometimes even decent. Nor is a pro-Negro position remarkably liberal for a Negro. Solidarity of the various communities is sensible but it is not especially noble. Most magazines, like most people, merely want to look good.

In another great war of the magazines, the champion on one side is the *Reader's Digest.* Here every piece is working hard to make a single, simple point, which is condensed in the title, which in turn is printed in the cover. "Modern medicine is wonderful"; "Life is good"; "Everybody is decent" are standards. The editors are clearly the nicest people in the world. And so we must be alerted when we notice that they occasionally print the complete opposite of the truth. For example, utility companies have long fought a united war to avoid putting transmission lines underground. But the *Reader's Digest* (November, 1967) says that utilities *like* to put transmission lines underground. In the same issue is a piece saying that local citizens can indeed sway highway commissions; another saying that very few kids use drugs; another that the Vietcong don't really want to fight. All these must be read as trying to persuade the wicked to change their ways. Perhaps this sort of thing works, though probably not on the Vietcong. This magazine is perfectly clear about the point of living.

The champion of the other side is *The New Yorker.* I trace its present, and generally misunderstood, character to about 1930, when John O'Hara, then a practical joker, contributed very brief stories or vignettes, resembling tape recordings (when they didn't exist), that had no point. Since life itself seems pointless, the reader was charmed and was obliged to invent his own point to the story. The magazine was automatically one up on the reader. Other writers contributed the same sort of thing, which was marvelously easy to do, and then the genre disappeared. The late Harold Ross had discovered his formula. Soon the whole magazine was saying that there is no point to anything.

For example, if you ask how many apples I have, I say in the conventional civilized formula that I have ten apples. On *The New Yorker* this is forbidden. No matter how often you ask. I have five apples and three apples and two apples, never ten apples. And for perfect accuracy I must tell you how I got them, from whom, when, and what kinds they are, and something about the historical background of apples. How many apples? "Five and three and two apples." This style cannot always be enforced on serialized books by outsiders.

For example (September 16, 1967) under the pointless heading of "Our Far-Flung Correspondents" is an interminable piece about lake fishing around far-flung Salisbury, Connecticut. It had no discernible point except perhaps that trout will eat alewives. Elsewhere in the issue were pointless inquiries into collecting old science-fiction magazines (but not reading them) and the invented company names on New York taxicab doors, checked and double-checked with phlegmatic accuracy.

We can see that Harold Ross admired the fable of the Emperor's clothes (my favorite) but instead of becoming the child on the sidewalk, the magazine brilliantly chose to become the Emperor with his exquisite, costly clothes, elaborately woven from nothing. The plasticity of pointlessness is such that it can easily accept existentialism, nihilism, psychedelism, McLuhanism, pacifism, structuralism, anything. Somebody there realized that the greatest discovery of the West was the zero, borrowed originally from India, the nation of pointlessness. Put after any number, it does wonders.

This stuff may fairly be charged with having demoralized America's middlebrows. When these people, confronted with problem children, saw themselves as pointless characters in a *New Yorker* story, they gave up. The subtlest subversion in America is certainly in this magazine, with its unexplicit message that everything is created equal, equally nonsignificant. However, very few *New Yorker* editors have committed suicide, so that the philosophy of pointlessness must have some psychic nutrition. The position, "We don't know anything important, but we're infallible," must have some power, perhaps trivial, but irresistible. Furthermore, *The New Yorker* has what is probably the largest inventory of unused prose and cartoons in the world, and since it pays well and in advance of publication, it spreads much happiness among unpublished workers.

The final clue to *The New Yorker* would be its rejects. John Cheever, normally a *New Yorker* writer, suddenly has a story (presumably rejected by *The New Yorker*) in the January 1968 *Playboy*. It is a beautiful story, "The Yellow Room," but it has a point: in fact, it is an odyssey with a happy ending, and several morals. In *The New Yorker*, it would be shocking, but the editor's explanation of why would probably not be that given above.

Esquire tries to be a coruscating sublimation of *The New Yorker*, but it has misread the inscrutable signal. Its happiest moments come in playing practical jokes on its readers, like its so-called Establishment charts, or its nomination of an unknown Indianian as the ideal Republican presidential candidate, not the infallible way to keep friends.

After a few of these, the fearful reader just doesn't believe anything he sees in *Esquire*, and so perhaps he receives a deformed version of *The New Yorker*'s subtle pointlessness, though he can never be sure. The reader's ego and superego are fighting for their lives. This may be a useful challenge. For people who cannot otherwise justify their lives, it may be good to find out whether they can outwit the editors of *Esquire*, in the fashion of a difficult crossword puzzle. *Esquire* too presents a great truth about life: everybody may be lying, and, some of the time, probably is. *Esquire* inspires a healthy paranoia.

Pointlessness (once, incidentally, the style of the English upper classes) is creeping all through the magazine world. In a very quick survey, I found these: Turin was originally named Julia Tourinorum (*Holiday*, February 1968). An earlier *Holiday* announced that one does not say Swiss cheese; it is

Switzerland cheese. "As a gas, helium is a remarkably uninteresting element" (*Scientific American,* August 1967). "Texas rat" is used-car cant for a car owned by a long-distance driver; and in Ireland, Bushmill's is "protestant whisky" (*Esquire,* March 1968). Taxis in Avoriaz, France, are sleighs with reindeer (*Look,* February 6, 1968). I cannot imagine what use I can make of any of this information, which may be correct. Except Turin, whose original name is given elsewhere as Augusta Taurinorum.

Perhaps this material is a symptom of the Ph.D. syndrome. The personnel are all narrow specialists. Much lip service is given interdisciplinary or multidisciplinary analysis, but the fashion still favors the specialist, who can be wildly wrong.

Two other opposites are the cerebrals and the carnals. The intellectual magazines run many pointed articles, whose chief fault is that when they seem to have about ended, they have just begun. The latter half of these pieces treats the tentative conclusions of the first half as solid major premises and moves on to more dubious syllogisms. Such monologues tend to become soliloquies. And of course they leave a wake of ruined heroes. One such article, on the social and sexual status of James Joyce, deduced his cowardice from the fact that he attributed his own obscene thoughts to Bloom instead of Daedalus in *Ulysses.*

On the other side are publications that ostensibly glorify the female body, which is not quite all that the female has to offer. The repetition of the splendid mammaries, buttocks, navels, and throats ends by making a beautiful creature as replaceable as a paper napkin. What in the world does anybody think healthy young men do in the presence of a luscious gatefold? Why, of course. They masturbate. They thus escape a little way from the power of the actual young women they know, who are probably not as well endowed as the gatefold lady. Thus, when a living, breathing woman takes her clothes off, their reaction is more likely to tend toward the dilettantish. Thus the "men's magazines" to some degree emasculate the men.

Playboy combines the carnal and cerebral with an official

Philosophy, viz., that pleasure is better than pain. The real question is in which sequence the two are experienced. The pain-pleasure sequence has always been recommended. "Have fun now; pay later" has been ascribed to the devil; the place where one normally paid later was hell. The theology is obsolete, the sequence is not. Pleasure-first has real hells.

These magazines may have helped persuade women to progressively denude themselves. Whether this is good or bad it far outside the province of this study. But this self-exposure certainly helps deflate the ancient drama of the female. The destruction of the old marvelous, or foolish, tensions may delight the psychiatrists and marriage counselors. But I know enough not to express an opinion, or even to have one.

In terms of effective magazine formulae, one must notice that one group of magazines appears to publish just by breathing regularly. This would include the *Reader's Digest, Life, Time, Newsweek, The New Yorker, Ladies Home Journal, Holiday.* Others, which are sometimes more interesting, seem to have to make a superhuman effort with each issue —*The Saturday Evening Post, Look, Esquire, McCall's, Harper's.* (These groups change; the *Post* used to be in the first group.) It is silly to say that the former fill pre-sold reader needs. With the exception of *Life* (an instant success) none filled any particular need when it was founded. They built a formula acceptance and are now running on momentum.

The magazines obviously try to report the current state of American society. The results of their efforts can be readily summarized: the city cum ghetto is the norm; the country is an escape luxury fit only for recreation and conservation; all the old allegiances (family, elders, God, race, job, community, nation) *appear* to have a case of galloping caries; hence, the old virtues *appear* to be so much debris. Of course, the old values fight silently for themselves. Some put up a defeatist counterpropaganda, as in a piteous *Reader's Digest* piece saying that wives are useful. Surely a more passionate defense of the old order is permissible.

Spokesmen for the more dissolute youth, in magazines I

don't read, embrace the dissolutions as heralds of a marvelous new world, where every idiot will be a genius. (Name your own: Andy Warhol, Allen Ginsberg, etc.) But the symptoms described by these magazines are contained in an old historical word: "decadence." The more heavy-handed intellectuals describe the American society as one of "madness, barbarism, tyranny, exile, grief, and ruin," that is, something far gone beyond decadence. Only one word describes anything I have ever witnessed—"grief," to which I am not, unfortunately, immune. People who can gibber so have got to be in self-made padded cells, from which they never emerge into the light where the sun also rises, the birds do sing, and the warm rain falls straight down. But this gibbering is high style just now.

Let us turn from the propaganda to the reality. In fact, America is not at all decadent. It might be theorized that a genuine democracy could never be decadent, in the old historical sense. The competition is too fierce; the replacements for the dropouts and fainéants are too ambitious, talented, and numerous (the most recent being gifted Negroes). The "new men," as in Tudor times, tear the old failures apart and trample over the young dilettantes, blinded by their hair-falls and their college degrees (not to mention pot and LSD).

In my day in college there was a category that would now be called jerks. Today they have a miraculous solution; they let their head and chin hair grow, never bathe and adopt the style. They are no longer jerks, but a great social phenomenon, bless them.

What can be said is that a youthful explosion of nerve has caused an adult failure of nerve, widely whimpered in the magazines. A lot of Chicken Littles are naturally crying, "The sky is falling." Some dead leaves, as of sexual, parental, racial, etc. relationships, may well be falling, but tomorrow morning everybody's got to get up, and start work on the next issue.

Also, it can certainly be argued that the magazines are disseminating confusion, since most people read more than one magazine. But we should keep in mind that the voices of the magazines—their language—have less to do with syntax, semantics, or even substance than with that elusive quality, style, which is the key to the clichés they trade in. Of the magazines summarized above, the basic clichés can be crudely condensed, in order, as follows: "Life is facts," "Life is whee!" "Life is earnest," "Life is pointless," "Life is a lie," "Life is a syllogism," "Life is pleasure." Only two of these, whee! and pleasure, are reconcilable, and they are addressed to different sexes.

The principal fungus in the society is probably pointlessness, the idiotic keening, "Where is it happening?" For the Happening is usually pointless and silly, and much energy is given to making the next, competitive Happening even sillier. Everyone should know that where it's really happening is inside himself. The culture seems to be intent on producing a running satire on itself. The only Americans who have a convinced purpose in life, without any apology, are professional baseball and football players, and some of these are suspect to the fans.

The decisive criticism of American magazines is that they are not laughing loudly, at the young militants, the Jet Set, the politicians, Madison Avenue, and perhaps themselves.

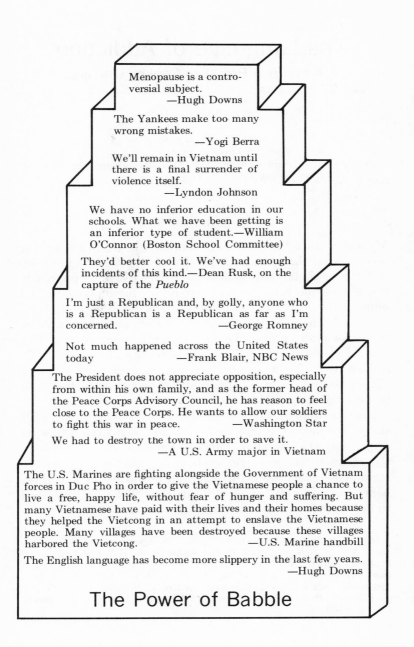

Menopause is a controversial subject.
—Hugh Downs

The Yankees make too many wrong mistakes.
—Yogi Berra

We'll remain in Vietnam until there is a final surrender of violence itself.
—Lyndon Johnson

We have no inferior education in our schools. What we have been getting is an inferior type of student.—William O'Connor (Boston School Committee)

They'd better cool it. We've had enough incidents of this kind.—Dean Rusk, on the capture of the *Pueblo*

I'm just a Republican and, by golly, anyone who is a Republican is a Republican as far as I'm concerned.
—George Romney

Not much happened across the United States today
—Frank Blair, NBC News

The President does not appreciate opposition, especially from within his own family, and as the former head of the Peace Corps Advisory Council, he has reason to feel close to the Peace Corps. He wants to allow our soldiers to fight this war in peace.
—Washington Star

We had to destroy the town in order to save it.
—A U.S. Army major in Vietnam

The U.S. Marines are fighting alongside the Government of Vietnam forces in Duc Pho in order to give the Vietnamese people a chance to live a free, happy life, without fear of hunger and suffering. But many Vietnamese have paid with their lives and their homes because they helped the Vietcong in an attempt to enslave the Vietnamese people. Many villages have been destroyed because these villages harbored the Vietcong.
—U.S. Marine handbill

The English language has become more slippery in the last few years.
—Hugh Downs

The Power of Babble

The Language of Addiction
Talking in a Pressure-Cooker Universe

Seymour Fiddle

Something's got to give
Was our pimping motto
As we headed South to the Border
In my black El Dorado.[1]

General Introduction

My argument is that the oral language of a group reflects the pressures on that group. In particular the speech of the addicted in a ghetto area indicates, copes with, and apparently transforms the pressure on their lives. But it overlaps and blurs with the language of those who while not addicted interact with them. This is the first difficulty that faces us when we wish to examine the distinctive nature of addict slang. I am writing here primarily of those addicted to heroin in New York City's ghetto areas and only secondarily about those who use "the pills," the suburban dwellers who may well be developing their own distinctive vocabulary.

A second difficulty is that many sources contribute to addict slang. The addict learns first from his own experiences on drugs. But the addicted generally have to have recourse to the criminal sphere to get their money so that we have to include as addict words, words used by people in jail. If we hear "jailhouse talk" we are not surprised. The man who refers to one year in jail as a *bullet;* two years as a *deuce* or a *due*

---

[1] An anonymous addict *toast* or poem, "Cocaine Smitty and Longshoe Sam," from a collection made by the author in the course of research on drug addiction. For a further discussion of some of the points underlying this paper and a brief description of the author's methods of research during the past seven years as research sociologist for Exodus House in New York City see Fiddle, S., *Portraits from a Shooting Gallery,* Harper & Row, 1967 passim esp. pp. 55–71.

(an Italian word); a *trey* (*tre*) for three; a *pound* or *nickel* for five; and a *dime* for ten is sharing a vocabulary with nonaddicted criminals. But such words cannot be excluded from a glossary of addiction.

Part of the addicted pattern consists in frequent recourse to hospitals so that understandably words from a pseudo-medical vocabulary appear. *Joy juice* means chloral hydrate, appetizers, tonics, etc.

Since many addicts admire jazz and there is a running association between some of them and some addicted or formerly addicted musicians, then we would expect that words from jazz would obtrude in the addict world. In fact a word like *gig*, stemming from the word used by successful musicians for a booking and by less successful ones for a weekend pickup date, is used to mean a job. I have heard it much more frequently than the words *slave* and *haim*, which some men used particularly for a routine job. Some words that are from music undergo change. *Jive* music meant good music but among the addicts as other ghetto people *jive* means phony. A word like *cool*, referring to a style of music, means something different among the addicts. A cool street is one where the police are relatively absent. A cool person is one who is with it, etc.[2] *Hot jazz* means one thing, a hot situation is a dangerous one, etc.

Finally there is the ghetto itself, formerly called the slum in less riotous times. Here the element which is common both to the ghetto and to addiction—massive social and personal pressure—makes it easy for words to infiltrate and percolate between both spheres. Words for knife, such as *blade* and *shank*, are used by people off and on drugs on the street. Words from the teen life, such as *boss*, can be heard all around the ghetto. If you hear the word *piece* you will have to wait to find out whether it refers to a gun, a woman, or an ounce of drugs. This intrinsic ambiguity, the fact that there is so much overlapping and blurring in the cultural spheres

[2] The opposite of *cool* is *uncool*, referring to someone who betrays a situation by his manner.

within the ghetto, is often cited as a source of protection, real or imaginary, to the addicted.

It follows that I am not going to be concerned about the origins of words because in most cases it would be fruitless to try to establish them. Nor in most cases am I going to say that the particular words I will examine are exclusively addict words. My only contention is that these words are used quite often by the addicted, and I suspect that if a word is going to be used by this group it will gradually take on specialized, even distorted, meanings.

The addict is subject to massive continuous pressure. First there are the police, who are much more visible in the ghetto area than in most other neighborhoods. The fact that the addict has to consort with criminals and that he himself is likely to be a criminal makes him a vulnerable target for the police for many reasons. He may be a robbery suspect. He may have information on gambling and prostitution. In any case because of the pain of withdrawal and his poverty, many policemen treat him as an easy victim. There is pressure from the drug hierarchy. The addict is a kind of proletarian in an illegal class system whose illegal capitalists are the Mafia, renegades, related criminal misadventure capitalists, and "respectable elements" who help bankroll illegal activities for profit. Since the drug hierarchy is profit- and power-minded the addict is objectively exploited by them. Thirdly, there is the *legit* society outside and inside the ghetto area. The addict feels their stereotypes and while he will make fun of them nonetheless he experiences popular contempt as a kind of pressure upon him. There is the pressure that comes from competing with other addicted men for money or heroin or prestige or information. Much of this is denied by some of the addicted but objective evidence suggests that there are these intersecting markets which in fact form the very heart of addict life. Finally there is the diffuse pressure that comes from living a life without a future that they can call their own and a present which puts them between powerful outer laws and equally powerful inner psychochemical drives.

How Addict Slang Generally Reveals Pressure

If there is a considerable amount of violent imagery in the words used by a group, we can assume that they are under general, intensive pressure.[3]

Consider the phrase *he was creaming*. A man uses it to describe his sexually excited reaction to a girl. *Dig that dude creamin' behind that flick of a broad* means *look how that fellow is aroused by the sight of a woman in a photograph*. He also will use it for someone who is exulting at another's deep chagrin. *After all that shit he was pitchin' about straightenin' up, puttin' down junkies, I was creamin' behind his takin' a fall for dealin'* would mean that seeing a man arrested for pushing, one who had talked about leaving drugs and criticized drug addicts, made him feel deliciously happy. The metaphor, which is extremely conscious, expresses intense excitement by comparing the experience of love or *resentment* to an orgasm, the whole organism climaxing in seminal emission in the presence of the observer. Pleasure is registered in orgiastic force.

Or consider the word *hang*. By itself it refers to a pattern of leisure of teenagers and adults (usually male) of sitting around or standing around a corner. The phrase is not, hang around, but *hang*. ("Whatcha doin'?" "I was hangin'.") To *hang up* is a term specifically referring to a pattern of committing or attempting to commit suicide in jail by using a belt. Here the phrase is not to hang but to *hang up*. To *hang it up*, however, means to give up some way of life or some means of self-support. To *hang up one's parole* means generally not to report and thereby forfeit privileges. It is the death of his rights as a free man on his own gallows. Finally a man may *hang some paper*, which is one of the synonyms to mean that he forges checks. The grim comparison between a paperhanger

---

[3] I leave it to the professional linguist to trace the verbal connections between pressure and violent imagery. I might point out, however, that in Italian one uses *lavorare a tutta forza* for *to work under pressure*, and *usar forza* for *to do violence*.

and a forger implies that the paper he distributes has as much real value financially as the wallpaper in a room. When a man is trying to kick his habit, especially to kick it cold turkey, and is suffering withdrawal symptoms, in some places he is encouraged to *hang tough.* To tell him to hang on would be too square.

Instead of saying, give me something, you say *whip it* on me, *hit me,* and an older generation would have said, *smash it on me* or *mash or mass it on me.* Shake my hand becomes *give me five, give me some skin,* or simply a hand outstretched, palm upward in a receptive position for a smashing hand of the other.

The word *bomb* in different forms has a number of explosive meanings. By itself it means a worthless bag, one that crashes down from an expected height. In the Spanish version, however, *bombita (little bomb*—called *bam* by Negroes) means an amphetamine pill. A bomb can also mean sensational news, news that *shakes everybody up.* A *bomber* is a long marijuana cigarette. A man who is *bombed* is very high on heroin.

In these and comparable phrases much of the resentment at being oppressed and under pressure gets itself out poetically. In a similar way the pressure shows itself in the barely suppressed humor to be found in many addict phrases. If a man has been working but also using drugs, he is likely to have been pilfering systematically from his employer. The phrase that describes the situation is, *he made himself a partner in the firm.* If a man is acting ugly and making dire threats to all and sundry he is said to be *selling wolf tickets.* The image is that of a man who is trying to convince others by his conduct that he is like a wolf. If a person accepts his threat as reality he is said to *buy the ticket.* If he challenges the danger of the salesman he is said to *cash it in.* Lurking behind these phrases is the old-fashioned tale of the wolf in sheep's clothing. The question that nags at the people in the situation is, is he a wolf or is he a lamb? A *football* in addict slang turns out to be a small pill of dilaudid containing one eighth of a grain of the chemical. If an addict buys one of these pills, he is said to have *scored a football.* The humor of hyperbole is not lost on the addicts themselves. The sacred word for a needle is a *spike,* which gives one at once the feeling of power as it is injected into the arm. But since the word for vein is *line* and the main vein is called the *main line* and the results of injections are called *tracks,* the whole picture of the addict's body is that of a railway system, his arms and limbs, etc. resembling interconnected tracks. Since opium was originally introduced by the Chinese who helped build the Union Pacific one wonders if somehow some weird historical joke underlies this imagery.

An addict who maintains himself by stealing meat in the supermarket is known either as a *ham snatcher* or, more colorfully, a *cattle rustler.* The latter gives the image of the addict being part of a Western horse opera. And if we remember that the word for heroin is *horse* and that the word for eating voraciously after kicking is *chucking* (derived, it is said by some addicts, from *chuckwagon*), then there is another kind of historical humor underlying this addict language.

The well-known way of describing a man's state of addiction is to say that he has *a monkey on his back.* Here the picture seems to come from the street organ grinder with his monkey, and the phrase suggests that the monkey who used to collect the coins for the organ grinder now collects them for himself. There are some men who are very fussy about the kind of heroin they will take and who spend a lot of their time traveling between different high-drug-use areas making detailed inquiries and finally selecting what they want. One way to describe such a man is to say that he is a *globetrotter*—which makes a world out of drug neighborhoods; another is to say that he is *chasing the bag,* which makes a pun on the familiar slang term for a woman and reminds us as we will be reminded again of the sexual connotations in drugs. Instead of chasing a skirt, he is chasing a chemical will-o'-the wisp.

Suppressed humor as an indication of pressure often also combines violent elements. Among the addicts a time-honored way to reject a compromise offer or an unsatisfactory answer to a request for heroin is to say *rub it on your chest* or, more tersely, *rub it.* Here the image is that of a man who tells another man to take what he has offered and to use it like mustard plaster. The hostility becomes evident at once to the man offering the favor. He is being told he is not an addict but has a metaphorical bronchial condition and should use what he offers for his own *cure.* The phrase *to run a woman* does not mean to supervise her, but gives the image of the penis as a sword and the woman as opponent in a fencing match so that *to run a woman* means to have intercourse with her. This is a synonym of the phrase *to jam a woman,* which once more flatters the size of the penis in a characteristic street fashion. There being a good deal of ambivalence on the part of heroin addicts toward barbiturates and hypnotics such as doriden, we would expect to have a mixture of humor and violence-involved imagery. We are right: these pills are known as *gorilla pills, king-kong pills, courage pills, bank bandit pills, gangster pills,* and *idiot pills.* The implication is that it is the chemical content of the pill which is responsible for the strange, erratic and dangerous conduct of the men who take them.

A third general indication that addicts talk like people under pressure comes from the frequency with which phrases and words are condensed, telescoped, and refracted so that only an intelligent guess can sometimes reconstruct the original form. It is as though the pressure on the addicts were expressed by deformations in their words. Consider the phrase *to round on someone.* This means that one has been listening to a conversation or engaging in it and decided that one has had enough. No dialogue is possible and one leaves. The phrase is a condensation of the phrase *to turn around and leave.* The fact that one rounds *on* someone and not *away* from him shows the aggressive element in what appears to be a merely passive phrase. To *cross someone* is a condensation from double cross. A *meet* is condensation of meeting, a place where one has a rendezvous of an illegal nature, usually involving drugs. An *old vic* does not refer to an English stage company but to an elderly victim. A *plex* is a stubborn, irrational attitude, an abbreviation for complex, which in turn addicts define somewhat differently than psychiatrists. Someone who does me a good favor *does me some solid* which is short for doing me a solid favor. A speedball is a mixture of cocaine and heroin, but the infinitive *to speed* is also heard.

The phrase *to take off a sting* and the word *sting* are dramatic illustrations of some of the complex processes of condensation. The mother phrase seems to be the expression *let's take off this thing,* meaning that one person is telling another that it would be a good idea to steal a given object. Then by compression this became *let's take off this sting,* with *sting* becoming an autonomous word and meaning either the object or the act in an illegal transaction. The vivid picture of the victim as a bee, with the theft being not of the honey but of the sting itself, is a distorted but perhaps eloquent testimony of the upside down life among the addicted. To *tighten up one's scope* means to get the proper feelings in one's head through the use of stimulant, depressant, or other drugs. The science-fiction image implies a condensation of the word *telescope* to *scope* but also somehow compares the body to an observatory. The person who is taking an object *to the shop* is taking it to be pawned at the pawn shop. Words like *splivey* or *splive,* used to mean that someone is looking good, also appear as *Joe Splivey* to mean Mr. Anonymous; in either case, they come out of the dark shadows of interpersonal life without any specific origin. The phrase *give me some splow,* like *give me some skin,* refers to the feeling of agreement or complacency or recognition and could be a combination of pow and splash. Someone who is entirely off drugs (including marijuana) is said to be *on the natch* with the word *natural* being compressed and used to indicate that the addict is aware of the distinction between the synthetic and the natural life. A very low quality heroin bag is referred to sometimes as a *skid bag,* which is a condensation of skid row bag. If someone knocks a man out he *offs him,* which is a contraction of knocks him off balance. But the same verb may be used to mean to steal things from somebody, which is to say to *take him off.* Finally many words are reduced to mere letters, *a*'s are amphetamines, *cb*'s are a condensation of *cibas,* which are doridens, *d*'s are also doridens, *pg*'s are paregoric, *h* is for heroin, *c* is cocaine, *gb*'s are abbreviations for goofballs, which are barbiturates, *m* and *ms* stand for morphine and morphine sulphate, sometimes cozily referred to as *morph,* etc.

Language As a Way of Coping with Pressure

If language reflects pressure and anguish, it also provides devices for coping with them. Let us consider a few of these devices.

1. Neutralization Processes

One way is to reduce the impact of square society and its morality. Words which have a moral connotation in conventional life are given a twist which reduces or entirely removes their immoral component. When such a word or phrase is used by the addict it has that much less threat.

Consider the word *righteous* with all its biblical overtones. Among the addicted it may be used to refer to a pusher who is considerate and honest in his dealings or to a bag which has full measure of heroin. Both the square word and the addict word have an affirmative positive tone but any sense of moral indignation is removed by the addicts. Again, the word *good* as in a *good girl* means not morally impeccable but rather economically profitable. A *good girl* is good because she makes it easy for you if you are her pimp by bringing enough money in for both you and her to support your *habits.* A man who is *treacherous* may simply have very flexible sexual tastes. A man who is *bad* is not morally reprehensible but dangerous. On the other hand he can have a *bad vine,* which is an excellent suit of clothing, since *bad* may mean aesthetically pleasing. A *fine girl* is one who is well built according to the average male eye. Someone who is *outrageous* cannot be accused of moral turpitude. Rather his conduct is either peculiar or extraordinarily lacking in good taste.

There is a parallel tendency to play down the gravity of addiction. The synonym for *I am addicted* is *I have a habit.* Not only does the word *habit* sound less controlling, but the very phrase *I have* as opposed to *I am* suggests that the addict is trying to make himself believe that in some way he can take off the pattern like an old suit of clothes. This is magical thinking, a point to which I will return later. Similarly, addicts will talk repeatedly about themselves as being *dope fiends.* The image of the *hop head* or cocaine user common in the thirties has been wrongly applied to heroin users. They know they are not dope fiends in that sense but by integrating the term into their vocabulary they mock themselves and neutralize the negative opinion of the outside world. The term also loses its power by the frequency of use. Finally, the bottle cap in which heroin and water are boiled is given a quietly domestic name: *the cooker.*

But there is a unique moral element. *To be wrong* is not to be accused of making an error in judgment—at least not directly. Someone is wrong who rats to the police. Correspondingly he is *all right* if he is trustworthy. Here a moral element enters into what is ordinarily an intellectual judgment and suggests one area in which neutralization is not used: the addict's relation to the police.

2. *Dehumanization by Metaphor*

Another way to handle pressure is to numb oneself to it, and one way to do that effectively is to try to act and feel as though you are a thing. There is a set of phrases which imply that the addict is treating himself or his fellow addicts as an object, not as a subject. Sometimes the metaphor is buried but analysis will disclose the dehumanized feeling.

Consider the phrase *I came in whistling.* At first blush this sounds like the very reverse of the dehumanized tone. However it does not mean what it says. It is used by an addict on entering a hospital in a parlous condition. Far from being happy he is in fact sick. His clothes are threadbare and full of holes. The whistling he referred to is the wind penetrating him. He treats himself like an old house or an old box with an old covering around and through which the wind howls, as it passes in the winter's day or night.

The phrase *I rolled in,* which is a synonym for I arrived

or I came upon the scene, applies to a man on foot and so the comparison is between the man and an automobile. Note that the man is responding to outer forces upon him. *Rollers* are policemen but in this case the basis seems to be that some officers come around in a car. If one has been able to lure another man's wife into doing what one wanted her to do, the phrase is *I pulled his wife*. The word *pull* underlines the sense of force and of the idea that the woman is being treated as a thing. The word *stuff* ambiguously refers sometimes to heroin, sometimes to homosexuality, and sometimes to a deception. If a man says *that's my stuff* in jail he means either that a man is his temporary sexual partner in the absence of a woman, or that he himself is really a homosexual. If someone is *playing stuff,* however, he is engaging in a con game in which the idea is to pull the wool over someone else's eyes and the stuff is the stuff that dreams are made of.

Mental activity can be compared to a physical map. Thus in the phrase *I know where you are coming from* a person means I'm not confused by what you say, I know exactly what you have in mind. Plans are compared to a map and mental movements to physical movements along the streets. *I know where you're at* in turn means I know where you are located psychologically or socially or in terms of your present state or your future plans. The physical location then stands for the psychological location. The process of understanding the other is perceived as a physical process of making a road map of alien places. On the borderline of dehumanization are the synonyms for remaining silent or refusing to cooperate: *go to nut city* or *nut up*. Here the addict is comparing the silent person to a catatonic who does not respond any more than an object responds to symbolic stimuli. If one asks why there is this hostility to silence, the answer seems to be that we are taken into a magic realm in which he who wants should get what he wants. It is a demander's market and in this milieu the noncooperator is felt to be alienated even among the alienated addicts. A mysterious example of dehumanization is the way in which the name *Jones,* standing presumably for the average man, means habit. *I got a Jones* means I'm addicted. This may be a wish that squares also shared one's life but the least it suggests is the way in which the average square is perceived as a robot and "de-animated" in this language.

Another way to dehumanize and cope with pressure is to compare the person to an animal. Women particularly suffer this fate. It is true that they are sometimes compared to things as in the words *tank* and *bumper* but it is much more common to hear them referred to as *bitches, canines, mustangs, skunks,* or *skanks,* and, if they are particularly attractive and smart, to *foxes.* But the addicted male does not spare himself along these lines either. To indicate that he is sexually hot and in ardent search for a female to sleep with he may say *I've got a collar* or *I've got a cunt collar* or *my collar is tight* or even that *my collar is so tight it's choking me.* Here the addict is comparing himself to a dog controlled by his mistress' leash. He wears a collar and is out of control and only his mistress is in charge. Once she releases him through the sexual act his collar will be less tight and perhaps even gone. So great is the pressure upon him, for example, when he leaves jail after a term in prison, that the addict colors the male-female relationship with a picture of a male dog and a female human being in interaction. A dog-mistress image dehumanizes—and castrates?—the usual idea of the active man and the passive woman.

A man is down on his luck. His shoes are warped and his clothing heavy with dirt. His family has rejected him. He can only sleep in the dark public areas such as the roofs or basements like an unwanted, homeless cat. Hence the phrase *catting.* The animal association reminds us how the hunted addicts jump over roofs and run down stairways to escape the police. Like the cats these *greasy junkies* depend on what the people around them intentionally and unintentionally leave around for them. Do they perceive themselves to be as independent and individualistic as the cat? If so they are partially deceived because many of them act parasitically and slavishly under pressure of need. The point, however, is that they compare themselves to a cat in a very invidious way. Note that the familiar terms *hepcat* and *cat* are simply nouns and synonyms for fellow or girl.

A *gopher* is not your conventional hole-digging animal. When he pops up in the addict culture he may be spelled "go-fer," a victim of a con game who "goes for" the gold-threaded story told him by the con man. The victim, believing he can *outslick* him, digs his own pit.

If a man tells his crime partner that they should *swing with the TV* when the TV is not their own property, he is suggesting that they take the set and make off with it. This ambiguous metaphor seems to compare the thief on drugs, haggard, snivelling and dirty, either to a monkey or to Tarzan sailing through the breeze with something taken from the jungle habitat. The reality for the addicted man is that he feels he is a hunter operating in a kind of jungle. He experiences himself as being treated as though he were on a more primitive level of human development. A frequent complaint by addicts is that they are treated like animals. But these complaints and this imagery are ways of handling abrasive contempt.

Magical Gratifications in a Pressure-Cooker Universe

If language reflects the anguish of the addict under a life of continuous pressure, then it also permits him access to safety valves from the pressure. It also offers him an array of words in which he can make believe that his goals are given magical gratification. Clusters of words also give the addicted in many cases a sense of magical playfulness and even competence. Together these functions balance somewhat, although I think incompletely, the effects of pressure upon the addicted.

Consider the word *mellow*. When conventionally used by nonaddicted persons about others or even themselves it tends to mean that they believe someone has matured out of his asperities and is now fully flavored as a human being, the analogy comparing a person to a wine. Among the addicted, however, the word refers to a feeling of totally complete satisfaction experienced by that person stimulated by anything or anyone else. The weather may be *mellow* when it gives a drug addict a feeling of utter tranquility. A drug may be *mellow* for the same reason. It is also the *mellow fellow* who is *groovy,* who does things to satisfy completely all those who evaluate him. The *mellow* thing or person is just perfect from the standpoint of the demander or consumer. Take next the word *nice,* which may be used to refer to a person or an act or a thing. The nice person is not agreeable or virtuous; he is one who is satisfying another completely; he is agreeable beyond agreeable. He is in short *mellow.* Now, a *nice* person may also play a game nicely, which means that he so plays his cards, so arranges his tricks, that he leaves his victims without any easy way of complaining. The burglar who leaves no rumpus behind is really a *nice player.* The con man who psychologically or socially ties up the chump or victim in such a way that he takes his lesson and does not dare or care to register a complaint to the police is a *nice stud.* He is perfect in making his demands upon the victim and pleases the observer who benefits from the game. The word *mellow* as used by addicts therefore projects onto the whole world a kind of beneficent climate, one which is utopian from the point of view of the consumer. The word *nice* takes the original meaning of nice and applies it generally to a man playing a game. In both there is a flavor of perfect relief for someone who is under pressure.

In a similar way the word *sweet* is applied to situations to mean that there was utterly no risk involved despite objective pressure from the police. A *sweet setup* or *operation* produces considerable profit with delightful ease. Often in describing such a sweet operation, a man will touch two fingers to his lips and kiss the air. Here the addicts have generalized from their dependence upon chocolates, ice cream, and soda as steady fare to a social situation. Perfection in a venture fraught with danger is equated with feelings an addict or any child would get with satisfying a sweet tooth. Pressure was expected and lo! *mirabile dictu,* pressure did not appear.

Other words like *velvet, honey, slick,* etc. form part of a small vocabulary of gratification that metaphorically serves to point the addict in the way of satisfaction. Through these cliché phrases they play at being happy and even being hedonistic. *Mellow, baby; groovy, man; baby, it's nice;* etc. are heard along with *crazy, man* in a continual, frenetic effort to convince oneself that this way of life is what one wanted all along and that the massive pressure-cooker universe really is not that unremitting after all. After all, in order to really be happy don't you have to have experienced unhappiness?

Although there are some men who get more out of using words than others, I believe that, in general, words give a kind of magical capital to the impoverished addicts. The addicts themselves sometimes offer another theory. When, for example, a man feeling his oats and in a mood to insult others refers to that *greasy junkie,* that *slab of bacon,* that *dope fiend, hope fiend,* or *pork chop* and everyone laughs, he will sometimes say that the reason addicts have so many words for the same thing is that they want to keep the police guessing. The idea would be that an informer or agent who is not up to snuff would betray himself by using words which are *played out.* There is something to this, I suppose. The officer who hears someone referring to *garbage, junk, shit, the white lady, the white stuff, skag, dope, doogie,* or *horse* may know some of these words but not others. But I think that the argument from defense is a belated rationalization. There is a pure play of oral gratification here and the magic that results, I think, is the magic of relief from the intense pressure of the life the addicted live and the prestige of possessing verbal capital. There is a kind of joy in being able to know that you can fall back upon *coins, edges, cloth,* or *papers* to mean what the ordinary *square* in his gray world means by money. Or if you are arrested you have the alternatives of *to take a fall, be popped, busted, squashed,* or *flagged* to say so. Routine patterns are given an imaginative and perhaps imaginary hue. One cluster of synonyms reveals how the addict's posture expresses his inner drug state. What do the following have in common: *tall, twisted, bent, blind, semi-zonked, blasted?* They all are synonyms for *high,* and the more eloquent the addict the more he can appear to have participated in chemical heaven.

I suspect that an analyst of Freudian persuasion would see in this oral magic evidence of a kind of dependency needs characteristic of immature people. At any rate, I think there is much evidence above that some apparent power accrues to the addicts as they create, manhandle, and invent highly unstable, ambiguous, and ribald language from a diversity of sources.

Curiously enough some of the very words used by the addicts suggest an awareness, however dim, of the magic of the oral sphere. The key phrase which links the mouth to the world of pressure is *ain't sayin' too much*. If a shot of drug does little to the man injecting it, he is likely to tell the pusher that his *stuff ain't sayin' too much*. Its performance was minimal. An inanimate mass is given a barely audible mouth. If in fact the one who uses the drug believes it has no heroin at all he will claim that *it's a dummy*, implying that it has mouth but is mute. Again the word *wolf*, when it enters addict society, drops its appendix, *down*, and means to threaten or menace. Eating and communication are thus linked. This oral emphasis becomes almost cannibalistic in the phrase *to eat someone's mind*, meaning to persuade someone even against his will. The talking process in some magical way chews off the other's brain. As a matter of fact there is what I would call *horse latin*, a branch of the language in which words are formed by the strategic insertion of the sound *iz*. This, I have been told, is also a defensive maneuver so that if an addict says *gizzive mizzee a bizzag of skizzag* he is really saying *give me a bag of skag*, which means give me a glassine envelope of heroin. How effective this kind of magical intervention is, is open to doubt. Watching the men playing at it, however, suggests they enjoy the game of mumbo jumbo it implies.

Magic of course need not be oral in reference. Consider for example the phrases *he got his wings, he shoots up*, and *takes off*. These are metaphors that compare the injection of heroin to the action of a man in a plane. *Getting one's wings* is taking one's first shot, comparing the drug user to a man who has had a course of flight training and passes his test. To *take off* and *shoot up* mean to inject the drug. (After writing these words I discovered that William S. Burroughs anticipated them. Speaking of his book *The Soft Machine* he says, "In this work I am attempting to create a new mythology for the space age.")[4]

Or consider the phrase *bust your stuff.* Here a man is in a sense telling another to have his heroin arrested. The police are at the door threatening to knock it down. The dealer and his *flunky* are inside, about to be arrested and sent to jail for several years if they are caught possessing heroin. *Bust your stuff* is an order or suggestion to throw it through the window. The police downstairs may catch it but all they may be able to do perhaps is to "arrest," that is, seize the stuff itself. In a way this is a magical hope because in most instances the police can connect the heroin to the apartment and thereby establish a chain of evidence to arrest the pusher anyway. However as in the other phrases just cited, there is a special value for the addict: magically he seals himself off from danger.

From Addict to Ex-Addict

If language reflects and affects the life of the addict, we would expect that there would be some change in the words used by a person when he leaves drugs. In fact, people who work in rehabilitation programs are likely to find that some words undergo metamorphosis. The new values of the addict express themselves in old words with new meanings.

Consider *garbage,* which, as noted earlier, is one of the words describing street heroin. A man trying to change himself in a rehabilitation program will ask for a chance to dump his garbage in therapy. He will be trying to offer to the group his emotional problems. The garbage refers to the buried gorgon within him.

One of the synonyms for pushing is *dealing.* In a therapy program someone is prasied for *dealing.* He is not selling drugs but rather he is truthfully and intensely probing his own present and past and hopes for the future.

[4] The reference is to the first Evergreen Black Cat edition (1967).

If an addict is arrested in connection with a crime, one of the ways to describe what has happened is to say that *he was flagged.* (This gives the picture, not often true, of the addict being in a car). If he is in a rehabilitation program and someone says *he is flagging,* the meaning is that he is indicating, intentionally or not, that he is looking for help because he has violated some norm of the program. The new picture is that he is acting as policeman to his own violating self.

Under the pressure of *the life,* a man will express his relief at finding a *sweet setup.* He means that he has a situation in which everything is coming in perfectly with little coming out of himself. In the treatment program the group will attack a man for *setting himself up.* He has let himself be seduced into a trap of his own by not changing himself and giving himself excuses for acting that way. Exodus House in New York City is less than a mile from a well known East Harlem drug area, 117th Street. When a man in this neighborhood is looking for good stuff and has connections outside the neighborhood, he will often say that he *is going to 17th Street* to cop. In our rehabilitation program if a man says mockingly that he is going to 17th Street, he is letting people know that he is angry or hurt or annoyed and that he wants to be heard. Seventeenth Street, then, becomes a symbol of emotional disturbance. And in the life the word *thing* might refer to *habit* or to something to be stolen, or to the penis, depending upon how the word is used and pronounced. Among ex-addicts *thing* refers to a pattern of behavior, generally one that is disturbing to the person and which he would like to change. If he asks a chance to *run my thing* he is really asking for a chance to set forth a *hangup,* and through its exposure to the group to begin the work of handling it.

Some Afterthoughts

In reading over the preceding pages I am chagrined at what I have been obliged to omit. I have outlined how addict language reflects pressure in its violent imagery, suppressed humor, and condensations, and how it mediates that pressure through neutralization, dehumanization, and various magical pictures.

But to do justice to the theme of pressure, I would have to show how addict speech itself serves to put pressure on many men to stay tied to addict life; how its rhythms and special effects color and reflect different drug states and their respective pressures; what the place of social class and ethnic affiliations is in regard to language development and how different life styles influence different speech patterns. We also need to study the manner in which sharing an esoteric and fluctuating language gives to many addicts a sense of solidarity which makes it easier for them to endure pressure.

Let me conclude by raising a broad question and making some suggestions toward its answer. What is the place of addict slang in the developing American vernacular in the 1960's and '70's? Does *slick talk* enrich the content of general American speech?

My immediate answer would be that there is little significant feedback from the addict culture into the wider American culture, and what there is is due to certain avant-garde writers and not to the addict culture itself. (Take the word *connection* as a specimen for speculation.)

But I am not convinced that the matter can rest there. I have a hunch that addict slang makes its effects felt indirectly, remotely and indeed obscurely through other groups and other agencies. This is a matter for research by sociologists and linguists.

Let me propose a model. There is a dominant though varied American speech pattern that in any region or area is recognized as legitimate. Below that there is a thin layer composed of complex speech patterns of those who are exposed to the dominant modes yet can function in some way within the deviant form below them; and at the bottom of the speech world is what we might call the *deviant infrastructure* including ghetto speech, the speech of homosexuals, criminals, addicts, hippies, juvenile delinquents, prostitutes, etc. All of these contain a common core of words with variations and distinctive word usages of their own.

I have the impression that there is a complex horizontal movement of speech patterns and words within the infrastructure itself. *Up-tight* has moved from the addict society to hippie society and out into the public domain. For instance, my limited study of those who are both homosexuals and addicts indicates that some of them feminize addict experiences and make a distinctive border vocabulary whereas others "accept" *straight* addict words and then reintroduce them to their nonaddicted gay friends. More research is needed on such border deviant cultures in order for us to study movement more effectively.

In the thin interstitial area can be found the police, who are obliged to learn something of the argot. Also found here are youth workers, prison guards, hospital workers, etc. We need much more research on what happens to deviant words in the lives and interaction of these interstitial people. Do words which rise become more rigid in the dominant culture so that they change in the infrastructure long before they change in the top layer? (The word *hip* is now used in the dominant slang as a noun and as an adjective. But among the addicts it is also used as a verb.) The youth culture within the dominant speech community appears to me to be most receptive to these fugitive and vagrant words and indeed is more likely to reshape them, competing in innovation with the people in a pressure-cooker universe.

Research on these questions, I suggest, will be needed to tell us not only what is happening to the American deviant's infrastructure but also to developing American general society and its speech. It will give us a special answer to the question one nonaddicted teenager in East Harlem put to another, "Hey man, what's the future?" He meant, you see, to ask what time it was.

The Language of the Law
The Lash of the Just

Stephen M. Nagler

Starving in the ghetto,
With the colored and the poor.
The rats have joined the babies,
Who are sleeping on the floor.
Wouldn't it be a riot
If they really blew their tops.
But they've got too much already,
And besides we've got the cops.

—*Phil Ochs*

The language of the law seems to many to be hopelessly complex. The codes, rules, regulations, and customs by which society is supposedly governed form a lattice of diverse shadings and meanings slowly but constantly growing and changing. There is a shifting balance of "freedom and order," "justice and power," "right and responsibility," which determines the legal relationship of man to man and man to society. Out of the balancing process come terms like *ordered liberty*. The meaning of such terms varies with the values placed on the scales at a given time. Employer and employee, landlord and tenant, creditor and debtor—all have conflicting interests which must be balanced to meet the changing needs of society. As Morris Raphael Cohen said:

> While some classes are doubtless more powerful than others, the law generally represents a compromise very much like a peace treaty. And in general, legal order depends more on respect for the law and even on the need to be ruled than on mere brute force. And as people become enlightened and critical, the legal order can prevail against violations of it through fraud, criminal violence, or rebellion, only to the extent that it promotes a maximum attainable satisfaction to all groups.[1]

[1] *Reason and Law, Prologue: My Philosophy of Law*, New York, Collier Books, 1961, p. 16.

To maintain "ordered liberty" and provide satisfactory results, the law must be sufficiently flexible to meet changing circumstances.

The importance of maintaining flexibility in the law has long been recognized. Lawmakers have sought, often unsuccessfully, to mold the law to the mainstream of human affairs at the same time that law is used to draw guidelines for activity. Thus, ideally, law is molded by the manner in which man normally functions in society, as well as determining which activities are acceptable and which are not. The repeal of prohibition is the most famous example of the manner in which law is guided by custom and practice.

But it is not enough for the body of statutes, judicial decisions, and administrative regulations of which the law consists to follow communal norms and customs. In a pluralistic society in which human affairs are infinitely diversified, laws, to be just, must be more flexible than prevailing norms and customs. Customs like old laws become entrenched while the needs of society are changing. If, as Holmes stated, experience and not logic is the life of the law, the law must take into account social, economic, psychological, and other scientific conditions extant in modern society. By noting these, law may both facilitate needed social changes and make breathing room for the nonconformist. There has been a growing tendency to do this in recent years. In *Brown v. Board of Education* (1954), the Supreme Court relied heavily on studies detailing the harmful effects produced by segregated schools in deciding that separate educational facilities are "inherently unequal." On the other hand, when the Supreme Court decided *Plessy v. Ferguson* in 1896 and laid down the supposed "separate but equal" doctrine, it confirmed a pattern of customs which had started to develop at the end of Reconstruction. By its decision in *Plessy,* the Supreme Court enabled the further entrenchment of the complex pattern of racial barriers which remain part of our American way of life. By the time the Court decided the Brown case, a tangled mass of judicial precedents, statutory declarations and administrative regulations had grown up and flourished, shielded by a mass of customs and practices from the enlightenment of modern learning and in turn shielding customs from enlightened change. So brittle was this structure that it could not be bent—it had to be broken.

The Supreme Court of today notwithstanding, the legal profession is still one of the most conservative and parochial. Most judges and government bureaucrats tend to follow what seems to be the path of least resistance and so continue practices and precedents which are most familiar if not most beneficial and realistic. Thus the process of conforming law to life in these critical times is extremely slow. Witness the ongoing struggle to establish meaningful scientific standards for determining whether a person is "legally insane." Did the defendant know the nature and consequence of his act, or, if he did, did he know that his act was wrong? This test, first laid down in Britain in the *McNaughton* case over many years ago has become rigidly imbedded in our law. Moreover, there is almost universal recognition among psychiatrists that the legal rule has little or no relation to the mental state of the accused person or his "responsibility" for a criminal act.

Also in point is the controversy surrounding marijuana. The almost universal legal classification of marijuana as a "dangerous drug" and the prescription of serious criminal penalties for its possession are probably consistent with prevailing norms and customs in the community.[2] But the available scientific evidence indicates that such a legal classification of marijuana bears no relation to reality.

But "legal insanity" and drug laws are only minor illustrations of the gap between law and life in America today. From urban ghetto to college campus, from lunch counter to school-board meeting, there is a crisis of confidence in the operation of government. What has been happening in the cities during the summers is not merely the result of a failure on the part of the legal system to comprehend biological and chemical

[2] How community opinion was carefully cultivated through an extensive but subtle public-relations campaign conducted primarily by former Narcotics Commissioner Harry Anslinger is an excellent example of how law develops through opinion formation rather than social need.

facts. Rather, there has been a major breakdown in communication between lawmaking and administration on the one hand, and social reality on the other.

For example, in 1964 there were 34.1 million Americans, of whom almost 15 million were children, whose income was below the poverty line. The definition of the poverty line is based on an "economy" food plan prepared by the Department of Agriculture for "temporary or emergency use when funds are low" and allows an average of seventy cents per day per person for food and an additional $1.40 per day per person for all other items, including housing, medical care, clothing, and carfare. None of the recent civil-rights acts or Supreme Court decisions has had an impact on this situation. Even laws designed specifically to reach these problems simply do not meet the need. For example, in December 1963 only 3.1 million children were receiving assistance in the form of aid to families with dependent children. In 1967, Congress, with one eye focused on economy and the other on the desire to "teach rioters [read "Negroes"] a lesson," imposed a freeze on the number of citizens who would be allowed to receive public assistance under major federal welfare programs. Countless others are denied assistance through the administration of arbitrary, technical rules and regulations having no relation to need.

Similarly, throughout our legal system, the poor in our society are subjected to a multiplicity of indignities which the law at best tolerates and at worst enforces. If they are Puerto Rican, Mexican or black, they are victims of discrimination as pervasive as that which flourished twenty years ago. All that the law has done in this area is to raise expectations without delivering results. Since the school-desegregation decision of *Brown v. Board of Education* in 1954, schools have become more, not less, segregated and the facilities available to Negro children have, on the whole, changed only by the addition of fifteen more years of deterioration. Discrimination in housing, employment, and other areas has likewise prospered through the indifference of governmental administrative officials. Perhaps the greatest advances in the fight against racial discrimination have been in the area of public facilities such as restaurants and public transportation. But of what value is the right to eat in a restaurant or ride comfortably on an interstate motor carrier if you can't afford the meal or pay for the bus ticket?

The cop, the magistrate, the welfare investigator, the public-housing administrator, and all of the many other government officials invested with legal authority impose themselves on the poor and restrict freedom to an extent unknown to the affluent majority. Of these, the police officer is undoubtedly the most widely recognized. The President's Commission on Civil Disorders found that in twelve of the twenty-four disorders surveyed, "police actions" were the "final" incidents before the outbreak of violence. "Police practices" were the first of the "deeply held grievances" which caused unrest. In its summary, the Commission stated:

> *The police are not merely a spark factor.* To some Negroes, police have come to symbolize white power, white racism and white repression. And the fact is that many police do reflect and express these white attitudes. The atmosphere of hostility and cynicism is reinforced by a widespread belief among Negroes in the existence of police brutality and in a "double standard" of justice and protection—one for Negroes and one for whites.

That police behave differently in white middle-class neighborhoods from the way they do in the black ghetto is obvious to any objective observer. In the former the police officer is regarded as a protector. In the ghetto, he is thought of as a member of an outside military force, like a soldier in an army of occupation. The difference in the manner in which police are viewed has deep roots:

> In the 1800's, when the large metropolitan police forces were formed, it was the Irish who filled the slums, committed the crimes and composed the police forces. And, says Pat Murphy, "the old Irish policeman in the Irish neighborhood wanted the kids to pull themselves up. He knew the people and he liked them. And he used his discretion. He didn't arrest for every petty larceny, but said, 'give the bread back and don't steal again,' which was and is good police work.

"But the second or third generation Irish patrolman serving in Harlem is not able to identify with the people. He may even be terrified of them. And he does not treat the kids the way the old Irish cop treated them fifty years ago."

But when confronted with a minor offense not calling for arrest—or when he feels certain of a child's guilt yet is unable to prove it—today's policeman, too, often feels called upon to teach a kid a little respect for the law right there and then. . . . And as we learned from residents of present-day Harlem, the policeman sometimes does his teaching with his fist or night-stick.[3]

In most of the South, the use of undue physical force against Mexican-Americans and Negroes has long been recognized if not remedied. The cattle prod, the chain, the fire hose, and the police dog join the gun and the nightstick as tools of the trade. The common and sometimes public performances of these violent exercises, with or without the collaboration of vigilantes such as Klansmen, are a matter of record. In the big cities of the North, the use of unnecessary force by police has frequently, but not always, been more subtle. When a man is shot to death by a police officer in the course of an arrest, arguments rage as to whether the officer used more force than was necessary. (This, of course, assumes that the person who was killed was the object of the arrest and that the officer had "probable cause" to make an arrest.) Usually a police officer is allowed to use such force as is required to effect an arrest. The use of deadly force by an officer, particularly where the person killed would have been charged only with a minor offense, punishable only by a short jail sentence or a fine, is particularly hard to justify. Execution on the spot dispenses with mundane considerations such as the guilt or innocence of the dead man.

Fortunately, the number of cases in which deadly force is used is *relatively* few. In a far larger number of cases the officer is accused of assaulting a citizen unnecessarily. Whether through bad temper, psychological maladjustment, mistake, or fear, many police officers use force where none is necessary or use more force than is required. Every police department

[3] Sam Blum, "The Police," *Redbook*, February 1967.

has its core of officers who have earned reputations for being free with their hands. When a cop *assaults* a citizen, he usually arrests the citizen on charges of disorderly conduct, resisting arrest, and assaulting a police officer. So regular is the pattern that recently, when a lawyer representing a man who claimed to have been assaulted and who was suing the municipality for damages discussed his case with a garrulous police lieutenant experienced in such matters, he was told that his client had definitely *not* been assaulted by a police officer. The lieutenant reasoned that since no arrest had been made, no altercation had taken place. "Look," said the lieutenant, "if that cop had hit your man he would have booked him for disorderly conduct, resisting arrest, and felonious assault."

Another level of police brutality is the problem of police harassment. Sam Blum interviewed a group of Negro men in Washington, D.C., who had formed a group known as "The Twangers" for the purpose of combatting police harassment. One of them told Blum:

> I don't mind getting arrested if I'm really breaking a law. But see that man sitting over there? He's been arrested three times in two weeks, once for littering—he dropped a paper cup back here in the parking lot—and twice for drinking in public. That was sitting back here behind the laundromat and drinking a beer, just like you're doing now. Now, that man has got a job and a family. He isn't a thief, he isn't a burglar, he isn't an addict. Is it asking too damn much for the police to leave him alone? But they harass him! They're just pushing too hard. They're looking for trouble and they're going to get it.

Insofar as our legal system is concerned, however, with a few well-publicized exceptions, there is no such thing as "police brutality." Any lawyer who practices in the lower criminal courts can testify that the only likely response to the mention of police brutality is the conviction of the defendant making the complaint. It is virtually impossible to have an officer arrested and prosecuted for an alleged assault or homicide. The uniform and badge seem to confer legal immunity. If two people argue loudly and are arrested, the guilt of either or both will be determined by the court, perhaps fairly. If one of the disputants wears a badge, however, only his adversary may be convicted of a crime, regardless of the circumstances. Moreover, among the human frailties that police officers are assumed by the court *not* to have is the capacity to lie. When an officer testifies to a series of circumstances indicating that a crime has been committed by the defendant, and his word is contradicted by the defendant, the officer's story will inevitably be believed and the defendant's story will not.

But the oppressiveness wrought by the detachment of the legal system from reality is even more severe than these examples indicate. As the Riot Commission Report states, the police officer represents to the poor a comprehensive system of criminal injustice:

> The policeman in the ghetto is a symbol not only of law, but of the entire system of law enforcement and criminal justice.
>
> As such, he becomes the tangible target for grievances against short comings throughout that system: against assembly-line justice in teeming lower courts; against wide disparities in sentences; against antiquated correction facilities; against the basic inequities imposed by the system on the poor—to whom, for example, the option of bail means only jail.

The benefits of preserving "law and order," maintaining police morale, and deterring crime are deemed far too sacrosanct to admit reality or justice.

In the private sector, the landlord, the employer, the retail merchant, and his credit company all have the weight of the law behind them. They are familiar with the processes of the legal system and with the men who administer them. Like the police officer and the welfare worker, they are outsiders to the community from which their livelihood is derived. Altogether typical of the manner in which law in the private sector creates oppression through its indifference to reality is the area of consumer credit.

Credit purchasing and the installment contract are familiar institutions in the American ghetto. Low-income consumers are virtually compelled to deal primarily with local merchants from whom they can obtain credit at exorbitant prices. The legal ramifications are clear:

> Most low-income families are uneducated concerning the nature of credit purchase contracts, the legal rights and obligations of buyers and sellers, sources of advice for consumers who are having difficulties with merchants, and the operation of the courts concerned with these matters. In contrast, merchants engaged in selling goods to them are very well informed.
>
> In most states, the laws governing relations between consumers and merchants in effect offer protection only to informed, sophisticated parties with understanding of each other's rights and obligations. Consequently these laws are little suited to protect the rights of most low-income consumers.
>
> In this situation, exploitative practices flourish. . . .
>
> Garnishment practices in many states allow creditors to deprive individuals of their wages through court action without hearing or trial. In about twenty states, the wages of an employee can be diverted to a creditor merely upon the latter's deposition, with no advance hearing where the employee can defend himself. He often receives no prior notice of such action and is usually unaware of the law's operation and too poor to hire legal defense.[4]

Under such circumstances traditional notions in the law of contracts would be laughable if they were not so oppressive. The legal concept that people who enter into a written agreement deal with each other at arm's length and are on an equal footing takes no account of one-sided "take-it-or-leave-it" form contracts, bait advertising, high-pressure sales techniques, substitution of used goods for promised new ones, exorbitant prices and credit charges, misrepresentations as to price and quality of goods, switch sales, or any of the many other "exploitative practices" which are facts of life in the ghetto.

Such limited legal defenses or remedies as are available to the poor are narrowly construed by hostile enforcement agencies and courts, and limited even further by the lack of access to legal counsel. New programs designed to provide legal services to the poor are wretchedly inadequate.

[4] Report of the President's Commission on Civil Disorders, pp. 275, 276.

Thus the legal system has failed for a substantial segment of American society. To the ill clothed, ill housed, and ill fed, the law means threat, not protection. The result is a failure in our legal system so profound and far reaching as to merit Pascal's description of it:

> Justice is subject to dispute; might is easily recognized and is not disputed. So we cannot give might to justice, because might has gainsaid justice, and has declared that it is she herself who is just. And thus being unable to make what is just strong, we have made what is strong just.

Stated in modern terms, the weapons of the law are all in the hands of "the man."

If, then, the legal system has failed to comprehend the needs of a substantial segment of American society and has thereby failed to effect a just compromise between the interests of competing groups, what is the predictable response? Thoreau's "virtuous men" of the 1950's commenced a long series of boycotts, freedom rides, marches, and sit-ins centered primarily in the South. Acting nonviolently against an entrenched system which resented all that they stood for, they followed Thoreau's dictum that "under a government which imprisons any unjustly, the true place for a just man is also a prison." Their demonstrations brought to the attention of millions of Americans the intolerable conditions which still exist and the systematic pattern of discrimination-under-law which still prevails in the southern part of the United States. Their acts and the violence which beset them evoked a response where there had been no response for ninety years. But the laws which followed brought more promise than fulfillment and left broad areas untouched in a system requiring drastic reconstruction.

As the demonstrations expanded into the North and began increasingly to focus on the injustices of the urban ghettos, allies fell away as the number and nature of the issues expanded and became more complex. The term *civil disobedience* became more widely used in a derisive manner to describe acts which earlier in the South had seemed more congenial (to integrationists). Many jurists now complain that there has been a breakdown in respect for "the rule of law." Their failure to note that the inadequacy of the legal system caused broad social protest has served only to widen the gulf. The call has gone out for new and stiffer criminal sanctions against civil disobedience. Commenting on recent events former President Eisenhower has said:

> Some of our leaders of both races tend to excuse such behavior. Not only is such an attitude extremely danger-ous; it sets back the cause of the underprivileged many years.[5]

Others warn that "we must avoid the mindless folly of ap-peasing and even rewarding the extremists who incite or participate in civil disobedience." This is the language of the legal cop-out. Lawyers who use this language are dealing with the manifestations of unrest rather than the underlying causes. They are like doctors who would prescribe decapitation for migraine headaches. Not only will repression fail to cure the nation's ills, but it will breed further violence, as the long hot summers have already indicated. The inherent conflict between democratic theory and the blind repression of dissent which will surely follow could tear our society apart. That "civil disobedience" by *government officials,* from avaricious building inspectors to malevolent police officers to intransigent bureaucrats, is taken for granted indicates the depth of the real problem.

The important role of demonstrations in pointing to sys-tematic injustice has been persuasively stated by Archibald Cox:

> Social protest and even civil disobedience serve the law's need for growth. Ideally, reform would come according to reason and justice without self-help and disturbing, almost violent, forms of protest . . . Still candor compels one here again to acknowledge the gap between the ideal and the reality. Short of the millennium, sharp changes in the law depend partly upon the stimulus of protest.[6]

[5] Former President Dwight D. Eisenhower, "We Should Be Ashamed", *Reader's Digest,* August, 1967, pp. 67, 70.

[6] Archibald Cox, "Civil Rights, the Constitution, and the Courts", 40 New York State Bar Journal 161 at 169.

As to the morality of compelling changes in the law through this form of social protest, Rev. Robert F. Drinan has said:

> Civil disobedience to laws that are deemed to be unjust involves the highest possible respect for the law. If an individual or a group secretly or violently sought to overthrow a law such conduct would be disloyalty to the idea of law itself. But when citizens openly disobey a law that they hold to be unjust *and ask for* the penalty they are saying in effect that they would rather be in jail than live freely in a society which tolerates such a law. Thoreau's words are applicable to these persons: "They are the lovers of law and order who observe the law when the government breaks it." [7]

We may speak of containing protest within the boundaries of the First Amendment, exercising the right to vote, and otherwise producing change through the use of more respectable democratic processes, but the "strange fruit" has been hanging from the tree too long.

Unless the law catches up to reality very quickly and the scales of justice are balanced, reality may be out of reach.

---

[7] Rev. Robert F. Drinan, "Changing Role of the Lawyer in an Era of Non-Violent Action", Unpublished address before the National Legal Conference of the Congress of Racial Equality (CORE), February 1, 1964.

Polluted Language

A New Linguistic Metaphor

Betsy B. Kaufman and Edward J. Lias

During the 1968 garbage-collection strike in New York, city officials worried that rain would cause a typhoid epidemic in the presence of the growing heaps of refuse. In the presence of pollution even the pure beneficial elements of the environment can become lethal threats to survival.

Pollution usually implies the addition of something to an otherwise relatively "pure" environment. When we imagine a trout trying to survive in the salt-water environment of the ocean (though the fish cannot recognize a pure or impure environment) we recognize the trout's inability to assimilate the added salt and classify the water as "polluted" for that fish.

If, however, some element is *missing* from an environment we do not think of it as polluted. A shark trapped suddenly in fresh water is in an environment which is deficient for him. A succulent plant would experience similar difficulties in arid land which lacks needed irrigation for life. Such land is in no way polluted but rather starved for lack of water.

In this article we will discuss pollution in its broadest sense, considering the effects of pollution on the environments of both body and mind.

We take as a basic premise the idea that each living organism can have an optimal environment which is pure for that particular organism. In our thinking, *pure* would mean that environment in which a cell or group of cells functions best. When a baby's "pure" environment changes so that a biological hindrance, deterioration, handicap, frustration, or lowered cell efficiency is experienced, he may (as a result of this pollution) get diaper rash and cry, communicating his problem in the only language he knows. A baby may survive with diaper rash but will be happier and healthier without it.

If we agree that each physical environment can be rated on a purity/pollution scale, then perhaps we can rate the environment of the mind on the same scale. For just as the physical world functions in an environment, our minds also function in an environment—the atmosphere of media and language. There seems to be no way for one person to transmit thoughts to other people apart from the various message systems in a culture. In fact, the mind may be unable to produce abstract thoughts apart from the media and message systems supplied by the culture. And without transference of thoughts, society cannot exist. Even in communities of ants and bees, studies indicate that elemental message systems and symbolic dances enable the relating of insect to insect, thus permitting the hive to function collectively.

Assuming that the mind could not function or exist apart from its environment, then the "purity" of that environment deserves analysis. What different adjustments will be required if the mental environment is squalid? Do criteria exist for measuring the contamination of the atmosphere which thought and mind must breathe?

Before we attempt to answer these questions, we must acknowledge that the pollution of one era may not be regarded as pollution in another era. When life first sprang into existence, lichens could thrive in an atmosphere of strong methane or nitrogen. But the plants polluted the very atmosphere which had given them a first basis for life. As the plants gave off more and more oxygen the existing plants debased the "purity" of the atmosphere; therefore a biological adjustment had to occur in order for life to continue. Man must watch to see if the linguistic purities of one time period might not become pollutions in another time or place.

In order to sketch our comparison let us assume that pollution occurs when any environment is altered from a long-standing norm, so that single entities cannot exist with optimal ease. The flow of comparisons from physics to language might be as follows:

A hydrogen atom can exist easily in a vacuum or in the presence of other, similar, atoms, but if its environment is "polluted" with oxygen the hydrogen atom will lose its individual "life" and will unite with the oxygen.

Similarly, the resulting molecule of water can exist easily in a wide range of environments but in the presence of certain chemicals or electricity the water will "break down," and change its mode of existence.

In life a cell can exist in water, or in the presence of other cells like itself, but in the presence of foreign cells or harsh chemicals the cell will deteriorate and eventually disintegrate.

Higher on the scale, a group of cells (animals, for instance) can exist easily in the "natural" atmosphere of air as it may have existed in 1700, but man's additions of heavy smoke, chemicals, radioactivity, and insecticide have caused a shorter span of life for many animals.

Presently highest on the scale, human social groups exist in an environment of media and language, each individual relating to other people via the "atmosphere" of media. But when the media are "polluted" the social "cell" will break down or disintegrate.

Which brings us to the fundamental question: *Is there any means of detecting pollution in language?*

Clearly the categories previously used in literary analysis cannot guide us in the quest for linguistic pollution. For instance, factual vs. nonfactual statements are not relevant, for either type of statement may be polluted. We all know how to lie with statistics (pollution by fact) and we also know how to win arguments with poetic license. Similarly, the categories of abstractness and concreteness, and ethos and pathos, are not measures of polluted media. Rather, language and media must be regarded as polluted when they decrease the efficiency of those functions for which they exist—namely to further the relating of people to people in unifying ways; transferring ideas with minimal tension and misunderstanding.

Which brings us to our first assertion: *Just as the inner organization of a cell is hindered by pollution, so also pollution in language will inevitably hinder the interpersonal unity of a society.*

No aardvark, for instance, can retain its inner organization with ease in the presence of pollution. Communication between the cells of the aardvark will be less precise, his heart and liver not cooperating with their previous efficiency. Hence the body must work harder biologically to retain its organization, metabolism, resistance to infection and so on. The communications between the parts of the body can be distorted or misunderstood in the presence of pollution, much as the Voice of America is "jammed" in order to prevent communication between the "free world" and the world behind the "Iron Curtain." (We are aware that these terms—*free world,* etc.—are loaded and probably constitute a pollution of language in themselves.)

This same necessity for communication exists at the social level just as it does in the body physically. Any two people in a community function and relate to it through the various media and message systems of that culture, *of which formal language is the prime medium.* Therefore, where social integration is lacking we should search for polluted language, for in its presence the social "cell" of people must expend more energy to keep the group intact.

Examples of social disintegration are available. Utterances like the following, spoken by Charles de Gaulle on July 23, 1967, may be samples of linguistic smog which could have dissolved the friendship between groups of normally friendly nations such as Canada and the United States.

> Refusing to be subject any longer to the prevalence of influences alien to you in the fields of thought, culture and science, you must have your own elites, universities, laboratories.
>
> Far from playing second fiddle as in the past in your own progress, you are determined to create and direct it and to get therefore the necessary teachers, administrators, engineers, technicians and specialists.
>
> Instead of letting outside concerns put to use your territory's vast resources, you intend yourselves to discover, organize and exploit them.
>
> What the French over here, once they are their own masters, will have to do in concert with other Canadians is to *organize ways and means for safeguarding their essence and independence next to the colossal state which is their neighbor.* [Emphasis ours]
>
> *The New York Times,* July 24, 1967

Most people would be willing to label as polluted all those sentences which prevented the League of Nations from being established, for they prevented the social "cell" from living with the larger vigor it might have enjoyed. But can we as readily sense the contamination inherent in the words of Charles de Gaulle above? He added in his speech that "this ascension of French Canadians was hailed by France with all its heart." We expect that all tensions between peoples (including black and white America) can be maintained only by a "noxious" use of language.

A second aspect of pollution is its effect on the sexual activity and reproductive ability of a cell; which causes us to infer that pollution in language may be apparent when the reproduction of thoughts is aborted between generations or peoples. In semantic terms, the "time-binding" qualities of language are miscarried in the presence of linguistic squalor, for contaminated mental environments handicap thought transferral.

If through language parents could induce their children to perpetuate life with *no* variance from tradition, culture would remain static forever. Fortunately this never happens except perhaps in isolated cases where language is used in a hypnotizing, authoritarian manner.

Innovation and creativity are normally the natural result of healthy thought reproduction, but in the presence of linguistic pollution, man often tends either to adhere too closely or to reject completely the way of life which preceded him.

Nearly all great discoveries are made because previous knowledge has been combined in a new or formerly unrecognized pattern or sequence. Wind has blown dust in people's faces for centuries, but not until 1901 did H. C. Booth reverse the wind to create the vacuum cleaner and get rid of dust. Even the acceptance of new ideas depends upon clear communication, for despite substantial evidence Copernicus was unable to surmount the semantic obstacles in the mind of his Pope and King.

James Watson, in describing his Nobel prize-winning discovery of the structure of DNA, noticed this phenomenon. He suggests that his inability to see the possible structure of DNA was related to the interpersonal relationships he and his peers encountered in the scientific environment. Linus Pauling made him jealous, Rosalind Franklin, the crystallographer, was too engrossed in perfection and in the idea that she had been given DNA as a personal assignment, and Watson himself admits to a greedy desire to be known as the discoverer.

If Watson and the other men involved had been willing to share their findings freely, the discovery might have been accomplished with greater speed and less agitation. Describing a lecture given by his colleague, Dr. Pauling, on the structure of proteins, Watson says,

Pauling's talk was made with his usual dramatic flair. The words came out as if he had been in show business all his life. A curtain kept his model hidden until near the end of his lecture, when he proudly unveiled his latest creation. Then, with his eyes twinkling, Linus explained the specific characteristics that made his model—the a-helix—uniquely beautiful. This show, like all of his dazzling performances, delighted the younger students in attendance. There was no one like Linus in all the world. The combination of his prodigious mind and his infectious grin was unbeatable. Several fellow professors, however, watched this performance with mixed feelings. Seeing Linus jumping up and down on the demonstration table and moving his arms like a magician about to pull a rabbit out of a shoe made them feel inadequate. If only he had shown a little humility, it would have been so much easier to take! Even if he were to say nonsense, his mesmerized students would never know because of his unquenchable self-confidence. A number of his colleagues quietly waited for the day when he would fall flat on his face by botching something important.[1]

The necessity of using intellectual energy for "survival" would have been unnecessary if linguistic problems had not forced Watson to view life through the "rear-view mirror." He might have, in a purer environment, been able to synthesize the concept of the molecule in considerably less time.

Formal language, of course, is not the only means of communication used by man, for much can be expressed through the nonverbal languages of touch, fashion, smell, ritual, etc. Hippies are able to say "I belong" through incense, drugs which give "instant" insights, and clothes which scream, "I do not belong to the decadent establishment."

The language of fashion, as a further example of a specialized language environment, can at times provide a wholesome "vocabulary" for global unity. The patterns, the styles, the textures, the design, the feel, the look of garments tend to cut across political and linguistic borders, providing a simultaneous experience for the peoples of China as well as England. Thus, regardless of the "language" involved, we are urging a

[1] James Watson, *The Double Helix,* New York, Atheneum, 1968, p. 36.

communication channel, the basic standard of measurement should probably be *the urgent need of humanity for global unity.* This implies that any message in the world which aids nationalistic, self-centered interests *at the expense of peace* and world federation is a pollution of language.

We might note that political language must of necessity be polluted to some degree because it serves to unify a group (small or large) of people who, despite their unity, cannot promote global unity until that political self-centeredness changes or ceases. In past ages, nationalistic language served humanity well, but in the shadow of atomic weapons it no longer serves. A global metaphor is necessary for survival today. In fact, universal symbols may become imperative. And we have yet to face those signals from outer space!

In his book *The Human Use of Human Beings,* Norbert Weiner says,

> Among primitive groups the size of the community for an effective communal life is restricted by the difficulty of transmitting language. For many millennia, this difficulty was enough to reduce the optimum size of the State to something of the order of a few million people, and generally fewer. It will be noted that the great empires which transcended this limited size were held together by improved means of communication. The heart of the Persian Empire was the Royal Road and the relay of messengers who conveyed the Royal Word along it. The great empire of Rome was only possible because of the Roman progress in road-building. These roads served to carry not only the legions, but the written authority of the Emperor as well. With the airplane and the radio of today, the word of the rulers extends to the ends of the earth, and very many of the reasons which previously prevented the existence of a World State have been abrogated. It is even possible to maintain that modern communication, which forces us to adjudicate the international claims of different broadcasting systems and different airplane nets, has made the World State inevitable.

The "language" of mass media, especially radio and soon global TV and computer networks, may serve increasingly to provide simultaneous experiences for people who would not

otherwise relate to each other. The ability to nightly plug
one's nervous system into the interests of the world serves
to promote global unity. Satellites which bring us wrestling
from   may clear
the   **DATE DUE**   f mental
envi   perish in
radic

Th   ore than
a req   o forbade
beari   eduction
of co   not prevent   "truth"
but v   , slogans,
synt   spite of
its "   e rancid
geno

Pe   ken often
enou   guage of
the f   hich will
foste   al "cell."